PRAISE FOR
WHERE THE ACORN FALLS

"From an idyllic boyhood in the '50s, through high school, college, a stint with the Coast Guard, and his professional life of owning and running "Salt Water Sportsman" magazine, he never stopped having fun in the outdoors with rod and gun. He writes with so much style and verve that a reader can't help but envy both his skill with the written word and the life he describes with it."

—Charles Gaines
New York Times bestselling author of *Pumping Iron*

"At times light-hearted, at times self-disclosing, Cunningham's intimate reflections on his road less traveled are filled with love, candor, and life's inevitable regrets."

—Harry Groome
Author of *The Best of Families*

"*Where the Acorn Falls* is a charming, nostalgic remembrance of simpler times packed with details and fond memories of a life well lived."

—Cort Casady
Emmy Award-winning television writer-producer
and author of *Not Your Father's America*

WHERE THE ACORN FALLS

a mental wandering of
growing up a product of the '50s

WHERE THE ACORN FALLS

a mental wandering of
growing up a product of the '50s

By Colin M "Rip" Cunningham Jr

Including excerpts from

AS THE TWIG IS BENT

being chronicles and anecdotes of juvenile
and medical memories, written in 1936

By Dr. John H Cunningham

Copyright © 2023 Colin M Cunningham Jr.

Where the Acorn Falls:
a mental wandering of growing up a product of the '50s

Colin M "Rip" Cunningham Jr
ripcham@gmail.com

Published 2023, by Torchflame Books
www.torchflamebooks.com

Paperback ISBN: 978-1-61153-576-1
E-book ISBN: 978-1-61153-577-8
Library of Congress Control Number: 2023912215

ALL RIGHTS RESERVED
No part of this publication may be reproduced, stored in a retrieval system, or transmitted in any form or by any means, electronic, mechanical, photocopying, recording, scanning, or otherwise, except as permitted under Section 107 or 108 of the 1976 International Copyright Act, without the prior written permission except in brief quotations embodied in critical articles and reviews.

This book is a truthful recollection of actual events in the author's life. Some conversations have been recreated. The names and details of some individuals have been changed to respect their privacy.

The cover photograph is of the author's son, Gil Cunningham, with his first Tihonet trout at the exact spot where the author caught his own first trout using the very same tackle and was hooked forevermore by his grandfather, John H Cunningham.

This effort is dedicated to my grandfather's memory and to the Old Farm Road gang who participated in the shenanigans and adventures that made life so exciting and interesting. Some are still with us and others have gone on to the next adventure. The grands are also a big reason that this books was written. Now they will know that even we old fogies were kids once.

n today's world, bookplates tend to be stickers affixed to the inside front cover. They were a little more formal in days gone by. I have decided to use my grandfather's bookplate as the description is still very appropriate.

The bookplate on the following page represents the source, the reception, and the expression of all knowledge. From each of the five special senses flows a stream into a common pool of knowledge-the mind. The human figures express knowledge in the only ways possible: through physical activity, sound, and recording by signs. The thistles suggest the ancestral origin of the author, the eagles, the country of his birth, and heritage.

Colin M "Rip" Cunningham Jr.

CONTENTS

Praise for Where the Acorn Falls i
Introduction 1
Prologue 3
The Early Days 7
Foreword
    John H Cunningham 20
I—As the Twig Is Bent
    John H Cunningham 22
Growing Up—a Little 29
Finding Trouble 37
A Little More Trouble 43
II—Plain Deviltry
    John H Cunningham 54
Other Pursuits 77
More Country Adventure 89
Finally Growing Up—a Little 95
More Time Outdoors 99
III—Maturer Outlets
    John H Cunningham 109
Moving On 136

More New Experiences 142
Outward Bound.. 151
IV—Forecasting the Future
    John H Cunningham 157
V—Observed in the Hospital Clinic
    John H Cunningham 166
VI—Overheard in the Doctor's Office
    John H Cunningham 174
Epilogue
    John H Cunningham 204
Back To School & More 211
Epilogue 218
Acknowledgements..223
About the Author 224

INTRODUCTION

Each of us has our own view of the world that we live in. Only you will feel the way you do and react the way you do. All of that is influenced by your family, your friends and your surroundings. There are many factors that make us who we are.

At the same time, there are many commonalities that we share as humans. How we interact with others and react to others. Much of this is what makes life interesting and perhaps frustrating. In writing down my experiences for this book, I recalled how I grew up in a place and time surrounded by family and friends. The impetus for these recollections was instigated by re-reading a book by my grandfather, Dr. John H. Cunningham, who wrote a book primarily for his three sons about his youth in Chelsea, MA in the late 1800s. Chapters from his book are interspersed with chapters from my book as are other elements from his effort. It is interesting that by chance we had similar curiosities and mostly similar outcomes. Having read his book several times, I was inspired to write a comparable title and record as many of my youthful events as memory will provide. His book was called *As The Twig Is Bent*. That name also inspired my title, *Where The Acorn Falls*.

Since, we had so many similar experiences and curiosities, as well as the sense of change from our youth to our children's growing up, incorporating much of his book along with my effort should give the reader a first-hand comparison. It will not be an exact match of chapter for chapter, but they will be intertwined in a way to give the reader a sense of similarities and differences. It is constantly interesting to me that experiences written about with 80 years of time differential can have such coincidence.

PROLOGUE

As I approach the daunting age of fourscore years, I am realizing that the finish line is a lot closer than the one at the start. I am also thinking back to as much of my youth as I can remember, and the realization that much has dramatically changed since that time is very evident to me. For my children, but mostly for my grandchildren, I wanted everyone to have some understanding of what it was like to grow up in the '50s in a relatively quiet middle-class suburban setting. In today's world, where we lived then would have almost been considered rural. At least we were on the edge of rural.

We, and I use that in the greater sense meaning the kids I grew up with, lived a fairly sheltered life. We grew up with people who were similar to us in most every way. We did not discriminate because there was nothing or no one to discriminate against. We did very little beyond our ethnic heritage. Our lives were determined by what our parents had grown up with and their parents before them. Something as simple as having a pizza was a real rarity. Bagels were unheard of. The most daring thing my mother would make in the kitchen was her version of Hungarian goulash. In many ways, we were sheltered from the greater world around us. My first interaction with a person of color was when I was 17 and in London on a summer trip just before going to college.

I hope to convey in the following pages not just what seemed like the normal mischief of young boys, but to give a sense for the amount of change that has taken place in almost eighty years. I say young boys because boys and girls largely did different things. It was not knowingly discriminatory or sexist, it was just the way it was. Also, to help the reader understand that what we considered normal pranks would now land the perpetrators at least in police custody, if not juvenile detention or jail. Yet, in my youth much of this would simply have been looked on askance. We never meant any harm by what we did, but of course we did cause some. Most of it to ourselves. The world really was different then, not necessarily better or worse, just different.

Much of what we did could have been blamed on overly active minds and some level of curiosity. None of it was done out of malice. A lot of what we did was due to the availability of all the things needed for our adventures. These are things that today are required to be locked away under penalty of law, which in today's world makes sense. There simply were fewer people back then. It should also be understood that we did not have any modern electronic devices. The first "computer" that I saw was in the Coast Guard. It was the size of a large refrigerator and had less computing power than your TV remote control. We grew up with the dream that Dick Tracy's two-way wrist radio might come true someday. Now we have phones on our wrists, but growing up telephones were only in the house. Many were operator assisted or party lines. Heck, we barely had TV. So, we did not spend much time indoors watching, listening or calling. We had to make our own activities and we were pretty darn good at that. Sometimes too good. We did not have parents constantly looking over our shoulders and all of this lack of supervision made us more self-sufficient and creative. We learned a lot from our mistakes and luckily our mistakes only caused minimal personal harm.

It was also a time when the police would actually take a stroll through the neighborhood from time to time. Certainly, the boys would tag along for a little while, impressed by the uniform and asking all sorts of dumb questions, primarily about the side arms they carried. From time to time, we tried to convince the patrolling officer to shoot any number of offending critters and even coaxed one officer to draw a bead on a large muskrat sauntering across the lawn of an empty house that backed up to the Charles River. No shots were ever fired, much to our disappointment.

In the last eighty years, a lot has changed. The suburban town we grew up in is far more densely populated. It has become more upscale or in the lingo of the day, yuppified. Again, I am not saying that is bad, just different than it was.

Plenty has not changed. The dead-end street I grew up on is still there with only one more house on it. Our house on the corner of Old Farm Rd and High Street in Dedham, Massachusetts is still there and has been well cared for. On the odd chance that I drive by, it looks in better shape than when we lived there. I look at the windows of my old bedroom which looked down on the vegetable garden and think about all the fun things that happened there as well as all the adventure since then.

I can only ask, "Read with curiosity, not criticism."

THE EARLY DAYS

Not everything in my early years is crystal clear, but I do remember all the details about the first house that our family lived in and that was 7 Old Farm Road in Dedham, MA. While I never did any research on it, the name of the street would imply that prior to becoming a sub-division of sorts, this was part of a farm. I suspect that it looked a lot different in 1900 than it did in 1950. This neighborhood was on a dead-end street that came off of High Street which ran from Westwood into the center of Dedham about a mile away. Almost across from the beginning of Old Farm Rd was the Dedham Medical Associates original building. So, routine and emergency medical attention was readily available and occasionally needed.

This was a street where almost everyone knew each other and just about every house had children of similar age. Since there was no through traffic down the street, the road was where most of our childhood activities took place, and our parents did not have to worry about our safety as long as we stayed on our street. High Street was another issue altogether. There was traffic on that main road and it moved along at a good clip. I distinctly remember neighbors losing pets to this traffic. The first we witnessed was traumatic. While we did not see the accident, we heard the screech of brakes and viewed the aftermath.

Sometime in those early years, our family got the first of a succession of black labradors. His name was Mike. I cannot recall his official name. Having a dog where we lived required a fence completely around the property and since we would leave the yard to play in neighborhood, we had to be diligent in closing and locking the gates. We did a pretty good job at it. While Mike liked everyone in the family, he had a special fondness for my father, because Father took him duck hunting and luckily, I got to tag along. Maybe that was why he never seemed to want to escape the yard, which would not have been that hard for a strong dog, which he was.

Ann English and Bob Mann with Mike, the Cunningham family dog, at the 7 Old Farm Road front gate.

During the summer in those days, we divided our time between the Cunningham grandparents' summer house in Wareham, MA, which was called Sandham, and the Soule summer house on Little John Island in Yarmouth, ME called Pemasong. We usually went to Wareham earlier in the summer when my sister, Terry, and I were young. That changed when we arrived at teenage years. While Wareham could be reached in reasonable time, something like 2 plus or minus hours. In the '50s getting to the coast of Maine from Massachusetts was an adventure in itself. It meant at least half a day of travel. Route 1 up to the old two-lane draw-bridge over the

Pisquataqua River at Portsmouth, then onto the Maine Turnpike to Portland. Then back to Route 1 toward Falmouth Forside. The family would re-pack everything into my great Uncle Orville Rogers' boat the Daiquiri. She was a beautifully maintained Chris Craft runabout with a perfectly varnished mahogany colored hull. It was just about the slickest boat that this kid had ever laid eyes on. Its gas engine and straight exhaust rumbled with authority, and I was sure that we were traveling somewhere near the speed of light as we skimmed over Casco Bay.

Thirty minutes or so later, we would coast into the dock at the northeast end of Littlejohn Island and summer had begun. Once we arrived getting the assorted duffle out of the boat was an impediment to scouting out the usual haunts and seeing what had transpired over the winter past. It was easy to imagine massive calamity, but the reality was that very little changed. Since Littlejohn Island was a long trek, you did not go for the weekend as is so common to many places today. We would go for at least a week, maybe two.

On one early trip, my mother had driven us up to Falmouth Foreside and Uncle Orville picked us up. Orville was married to my mother's father's sister, Lydia Soule. We were to spend two weeks on the island and my father would be up for a few days in the middle and then back to work.

The house at Littlejohn, built in 1878 by shipwrights from the family ship building yard in South Freeport, had a big wrap-around porch where almost all the activity took place. In the right front corner was a glassed-in section to protect against the prevailing wind and make the dining table area more comfortable. It was a perfect place for people to sit and watch the water world go by. It was also perfect for a dog to sit or lie and survey the activity.

When Uncle Orville came back from Falmouth Foreside with my father, Mike saw him get off the boat and not being used to the glass took off toward the dock. He got most of the way through the glass pane then tried to retreat. It was truly a bloody disaster. My father gathered Mike up and wrapped him in several towels. Still in his suit, he carried the dog back to the boat. Unable to find a veterinarian in the Falmouth, ME area, he simply drove back to Dedham and had Dr. Siegel, our normal veterinarian, patch poor Mike up. He healed fairly well, but it took most of that entire summer and required him to be kept with minimum activity.

The Soule family house on Littlejohn Island, ME as it was in the 50s and 60s.

Being on Littlejohn Island was a constant adventure replete with daily excursions to the post office for us kids. The tiny building used as the Post Office was on the town dock near the south end of the island. Since the Post Office was part of a small store, the nickel we would get for fetching the mail was immediately spent on candy or a soda. It was also a daily adventure. To get to the dock, we would walk down a path at the island edge and have to go through several turnstiles as some of the area was still cow pasture. The turnstiles allowed humans to push through the circular gate, but cows couldn't do it. The trick was to get to the turnstile first and charge a toll of a penny to get through. At the Post Office the mail was placed in a leather pouch with the family name, Soule, Littlejohn Island on it that we carried to and from.

When we weren't going to the main dock, we spent time on the beach. Having a big beach was and is a rarity for Casco Bay islands. Digging soft shelled clams was a constant low tide activity. In those days, almost no one paid any attention to the very abundant mussels for food, but we would use them for bait, if we went fishing with hand lines. If not on the beach, we'd be exploring around the north end of the island. There was always a lot to see and many tidal pools to investigate. At least once, while there, we would have a cookout lunch at the aptly named Lunch Rock on the opposite side of the island from the house. If our trip timing was right, we would be on the island when Uncle Orville would hold a clam bake for friends and relatives. Captain Harold Sawyer who ran the Handy Andy, a well-known Casco Bay workboat, was a god-like personage being the only one I knew of called "Captain." He lived in one of the oldest houses on the island, the farmhouse up the hill behind the main house. It was built in the early 1800s with wood milled right on the island. Harold would join in to help cook the clams and lobster. While I don't know for sure, I suspect he also helped in order to get some of Orville's cold beer. In any case, it was a festive event with all local seafood. One of the things that made life there so different was being on a real island. You were not that far from the mainland, but it sure felt like you were. In 1956, the bridge from the mainland to Cousins Island was built to allow for the construction of a power plant on the south end of that island. There was a rickety old bridge from Cousins Island to Little John Island. Suddenly it was possible to drive to the island. The first time that we crossed the old bridge between Cousins and Little John, my mother was concerned that it would collapse. So, she had my sister and me get out of the car and walk across first. The car made it on and off, much to my dismay. I somehow thought that if the bridge collapsed and the car disappeared into the mud, we'd have to stay for the rest of the summer. I believe that by the following year, a causeway had been installed and the islands were permanently connected to the mainland. It was still always an adventure going to the island in Maine, but with the ability to drive, something changed in the sense of living on that real island.

Being on Old Farm Rd was not so bad either. We had a pretty fun gang of kids. The Andresens, two houses down the road, had four children, the two oldest were girls. Judy and Daphne, being more grown up, did not join in a lot of our activities. I believe they were thinking about boys and not their brothers. But Spider and Winkie were constantly in the mix. Later in life, Spider and I became business partners in Salt Water Sportsman magazine. Spider was also one of my groomsmen in my wife, North's (Lyman), and my wedding. By chance, the Andresens lived next door to the Lyman's when they moved full time to Duxbury. Not only were we kids friends, but my father and Spider's father, John, were birds of a feather and spent a great deal of time hunting ducks on a wonderful piece of the Duxbury, MA back marsh.

Next door to the Andresen's were the Mann's. Bob and Ted were their two sons. Bob was always up for any adventure and was the instigator on many. Ted participated sometimes but was what we called "bookish!" Today he might simply be "wicked smart." A lot of time was spent at the Mann's as they had a large lawn area between their house and Mr. (Bill) Mann's garden. They had a tether ball set up and we would spend hours batting that around and around. Bob was a very good friend and was my best man at North's and my wedding.

Across from the Mann's were the Dunkle's. Their two sons were Bob and Peter. They were both older, but Peter was the closest in age and we tried to be friendly, since they had what was a real rarity in those days, a swimming pool. When we did get in to swim, we had to keep any noise to an absolute minimum as Mrs. Dunkle was easily disturbed and if we caused a problem, we'd be sent scurrying out of their fenced in yard.

Then came the Archibald's. There were 3 sons, Rick, Sandy and Bill. Rick was rocket scientist smart and played with us when he wanted to. Sandy was a regular and Bill participated when he was allowed. One incident with Spider Andresen and Rick Archibald sticks out. It was during winter and Rick got a new pair of ski boots. He was trying them out and wearing them out in the yard. Somehow, Rick and Spider got into a fight which would normally be a minor boy's scuffle with some shoving. Rick had seen or read about taking someone down with a leg tackle, not usually performed with ski boots on. He tried to do it to Spider. This caused the first elongated fracture of the tibia. And just for good measure he kicked Spider just above the ankle which caused a second fracture. Mrs. (Carmen) English heard the whaling and arrived on the scene to find Spider in tears. She told him to get up and get into his house. Somehow he did. Mrs. (Lallie) Andresen called Dr. Putnam who came right over as house calls were the norm in those days. He walked in and took one look and said that leg is broken. Spider was taken to Dedham Medical immediately. He had a cast from above the knee to just his toes sticking out. Every kid on the street got to sign his cast, except Rick. I am not sure they ever resolved their issue or even spoke again.

Standing - Ann (L) and Kim (R) English.
Seated L to R - Bill Archibald, Eddie English, Winkie Andresen, Sandy Archibald, Charlie English. In front of Andresen's house.

The English's rounded out the gang. There were two girls, Kim and Ann, and two boys, Charlie and Eddie. It may have been that there were 4 English's that participated in whatever activities we dreamt up, but we seemed to spend a lot of time in their yard, until one unfortunate act. Bob Mann and I found some shingles that had come off the roof of our garden shed. We discovered that these could be sent a long distance if properly scaled. So, we tried to see how far we could get one to go. I scaled one out of the yard and across the street into the English's yard. It hit Ann just above the right eye and cut her badly. She had to be taken to Dedham Medical to be stitched up and I thought that Mr. (Arthur) English was going to kill me. So, for quite a while, I did not go over to their yard to play. After some time, the whole incident blew over and we rarely scaled any more shingles.

The summer was a particularly fun time. In those days, after we had breakfast at home, we would be off for the day mostly without any indication of where we might be as our parents knew it would be somewhere on the dead-end street. At whatever house we were gathered at lunchtime, we'd often just eat something there. Our only obligation at home was dinner at 5:30. Being late was not an option. The other thing that was not an option was getting something other than what was put in front of you to eat. If you did not want to eat it, fine. But you had to sit there without a lot of wiggling until everyone else was done. No dinner meant no desert, if there was any. Our family and most of the other families in those days never went out to dinner at a restaurant. I do mean never. I am not sure how old I was when I first went to a restaurant, but I'm fairly sure it was not before I turned 10.

After helping clean up dinner, we were off again usually with a little jingle in our pockets. Sometime between 6:30 and 7, the Good Humor ice cream truck drove down the street to the end with his chimed music playing loudly and came back to just about the middle. All of the kids on the street would assemble like clockwork as if the Good Humor man was the Pied Piper of Hamelin and we were the rats. Even some of the older kids and the occasional adult lined up for a treat. There was a selection of popsicles, chocolate covered ice cream bars and creamsicles. Everyone had their favorites. Popsicles and creamsicles were a nickel and the chocolate covereds were a dime. The Good Humor man also had a very impressive coin dispenser hooked on his belt right in front. Coins for each purchase slipped seamlessly into the dispenser. If he had to make change for any purchase, he did so without even looking down. Dollar bills went into his pocket and change practically flew out of the dispenser. Unfortunately, my favorite was a chocolate covered and I might not always have the ten cents. At that time, we did not get allowances and what money we had was earned doing whatever was on the list of chores posted on the front of the refrigerator, which we called the ice box. Since our street was late in his schedule, it was also not unusual for him to be out of popular varieties. But we survived and were forced to try other flavors.

After, the ice cream truck departed, we'd be back to tether ball, hopscotch, capture the flag or whatever game we'd been playing prior to the arrival of the Good Humor man. That was when we had to keep an eye on whatever clock was nearby again. Nobody in the early years had a wristwatch. The second time that we absolutely had to make sure to be home at 7:30 pm to get ready for bed. The 5:30 dinner deadline was pretty universal with all the families. The home-to-bed deadline varied a little bit, but for whatever reason, our mother was fairly strict on that requirement. My sister and I were usually in bed at 8 pm. In the summer, there was still a lot of light left in the day and some of the rest of the gang would be out making noise. I distinctly remember that and the noise of the constant chirping of robins. The latter is a sound that brings back those memories still today.

I do not know why my mother was so strict on the 7:30 time. However, my father was a traveling salesman and was on the road most weekdays. He would put between 70,000 and 90,000 miles a year on his car. So, my mother had to cope alone with us. I did a whole bunch of things I likely should not have done during those years, but I never even thought of sneaking out of the house after bedtime curfew. In such a close-knit neighborhood, all the mothers knew what each household's deadlines were. If I made it out of the house, I would have been spotted and someone would get the word back to my mother. She might just give me a scolding, but when my father returned at the end of the week there would be more serious consequences. Being grounded, was one of them and that meant being stuck in the house or worse in your room for some long period of time. Remember, we did not have any modern electronics. A radio in the kitchen was it for a long while and that was tuned to music for my mother.

It was sometime in the early '50s that the lack of electronics changed. My father ordered a television through HeathKit. This required him to assemble the entire TV. I have no idea how long it took, but I do remember him spending a lot of time in the cellar. Then one day it was time to test the finished product. The knob was turned and after a little fuzziness and adjusting the rabbit ear antennas, there was a picture and sound. The screen was round and about 12 inches in diameter, but it was TV and the beginning of a new era. We got three channels. My parents watched the news and we got to watch Howdy Doody. Being grounded in the house got a little better. It was shortly after that when I got a kit to make a very simple crystal radio. It had no power, but magically picked up radio airwaves. It got a couple of stations and I distinctly remember listening to the Boston Celtics games at night after I was supposed to be asleep. The radio had a crude wired earpiece for a speaker, so I could do it without anyone knowing. For some reason, even with my constant listening, I never really became a Celtics fan until much later in life.

The old TV got what I remember as a lot of viewing. I'm not sure how many years it took, but whatever the fluid was in the TV screen tube, it began to leak out or evaporate. The fluid level got lower and lower. The picture was odd shaped and compressed, but we watched on. The good Lord only knows what was in that tube, but it would likely be considered hazardous today. We finally got another black & white manufactured TV with about a 15 inch screen. That seemed quite big. The old kit TV sat in the cellar playroom for a few years. I don't think my father had the heart to throw it out after he spent so much time building it. I know that I kept my little crystal radio long after I listened to it regularly. Trying it every now and then to see if it still worked, and it did.

My parents even bought another TV that they put in their bedroom. It was also a small black & white picture, and I am not really sure what they watched. I would often lie in bed with my father and watch the Friday Night Fights, at least until I fell sound asleep. The first color TV that I remember was in the '60s at my father's older brother's house. Uncle Jack was at the beginning of the migration away from black & white. It was nothing like what we have today, but it looked pretty amazing to most of us. At family gatherings we got to watch football games in living color.

There were other things that were common practice in those days that faded away and in the '80s were brought back as something new and modern. In 1989, Peapod home food delivery was touted as the new way to shop. Well, not really. Back on Old Farm Rd, there was Vitale's Market in Dedham Square. Rocco Vitale was the proprietor and head butcher. He had the finest meats around and priced them that way. A little later in life, he showed me the meat locker and he would hang hind quarters until the exterior was black and the interior was tender. If you wanted a melt-in-your mouth steak, you called Rocco. You could also call Rocco with your complete shopping list. He would fill it and deliver it to your house. His delivery method was a great old, slightly sway-backed, horse and a green wagon with a top and roll down canvas sides and the Vitale name prominently displayed on the side of the wagon. In those days, no one locked their doors, even if they were out of the house. So, Rocco's deliveryman would simply take the items into the house and put those requiring cold into what we called the "icebox." It was called the icebox since some folks did not have refrigerators, but still had the old-style icebox which required ice to be delivered and placed into the box. Both sides of my grandparents, the Cunningham's and the Soule's, had iceboxes and almost everyone called them by that name even when ultimately they were electrified. Rocco was not the only market that had this service. SS Pierce (pronounced "purse" by proper Bostonians) and Rimlees markets did the same. But only Rocco used a horse and cart to deliver all the way to the ice box.

We also had a milkman who delivered a couple of times a week. The refrigeration in his delivery truck was ice and I can still see the water continually dripping from the underside. Whether it was the ice water or the materials of the truck, it also had a distinctive metallic smell. On delivery days, you left the empty glass bottles on the backdoor step, in or next to the insulated box that the full bottles could be placed in. My mother would leave a note with what she wanted. If the weather was very hot and no one was home, the milkman would simply go in and put the order in the icebox. If I was at home, when the milkman arrived, and I wanted either strawberry or chocolate flavored milk, I'd just tell the milkman that my mother forgot to add that to the list. My mother got wise to the trick and would put "no chocolate or strawberry" on the list. If we worked hard, we could still persuade him to leave what we wanted, sometimes.

As mentioned earlier, during the warmer months the Good Humor truck arrived every evening. The mail was delivered right to the door and placed through a mail slot. Outgoing mail was put partially hanging out the slot. There were no mailboxes in front of the houses. It would have been possible to be a complete couch potato as all the things that are now considered modern conveniences were available and regularly used.

There were some other items that we sold door-to-door. At the Reed's house, we made pies, mostly apple and sold those around the neighborhood. Phil's father, Loring, had an interest in a small bottling company in Norfolk, MA. So, we went around the neighborhood as well as adjacent streets and sold mostly case lots of any of the variety of sodas that they made. I recall they made a very good birch beer soda and a sarsaparilla, which were somewhat similar in taste, but different in color and both favorites of mine. After we made the sale, we'd deliver the cases of soda towing them behind our bikes in a Red Flyer wagon. That worked okay for small volume, but as we built up the business, we had to have Loring make the deliveries with his station wagon. More on this later, but we used most of the money we made to fund our other varied endeavors.

The telephone service of the day was like the black & white TV, pretty simple. In Dedham, we had a rotary dial phone. Pick up the receiver, get a dial tone and one-by-one stick your finger in the correct numbered hole and spin it to the right until it hit the stop. There were no area codes back then either. In my grandparent's house in Dover, there was no dial. You simply picked up the receiver and got an operator, who worked over the drugstore in town. You gave her the number you wanted. It was only 3 numbers, such as 670. This also allowed one to have what would be considered the original call forwarding. If one was going to be at a neighbor's house for the afternoon, just let the operator know (in many cases she already knew, if she had listened in on the original conversation) and she would put your calls through to the neighbor's. At the summer house in Wareham, there were rotary dials on the phone, but there were party lines. Two or three parties shared a line. Each party had a separate ring. One long ring might be the Cunningham's, 2 short rings the Woodworth's, 3 short rings the Parker's. If someone was spending too much time controlling the line, there were all sorts of things one did to express displeasure.

So, while folks did not have all the current electronic gadgets to make our lives easier, we certainly did have some conveniences that all took for granted and that would, in later life, be re-invented as a new ideas. The very first editor that I worked for, Frank Woolner, would half-jokingly and half-seriously say when I tried to promote some new fishing idea, "There's nothing new under the sun."

FOREWORD

JOHN H CUNNINGHAM

THE following pages, written primarily for my boys, will convey some idea of the pleasures of the youth of my vintage. As I look back over fifty years or thereabouts of occasional but rather regular and varied outdoor sports, I am convinced that such success as I may have attained in life is due in great measure to home regimentation, friendships, health, and a better perspective regarding all phases of life which come as a result of those influences. I, therefore, am attempting to recall and record some of them for my boys, in the sincere hope that in reading these pages, they may share vicariously in the enjoyment and profit I have experienced and, by doing so, better understand why their "Old Man" has always tried to be a young man with them.

All expressed in these pages is but a part of each of the recorded subjects that have been enjoyed, presumably highlights, because they have been personally interesting enough to be remembered for one reason or another. Their appearance in book form for my boys and a few of my intimates is the result of a suggestion made by Dr. Hamilton Holt, President of Rollins College, who, as a convalescent patient, took an interest in them, saw, as he expressed it, "A proper record of the youthful impulses of a generation ago," and urged their recording. My audacity was further encouraged by my most appreciated friends, Dr. John C. Phillips and Dr. Francis S. Watson, whose contributions along somewhat similar lines I have always enjoyed. These friends seemed to see something worthwhile in this record and gave me the necessary confidence to present this volume.

Frivolous as much of the text may be, I hope that my readers may discover an underlying appreciation of the value of youthful energy (born chiefly of good health) and a definite recognition of the importance of parental discipline.

—J. H. C.

I
AS THE TWIG IS BENT

JOHN H CUNNINGHAM

*T*HIS volume is not an autobiography. I am told that an autobiography, to possess any value, must be truthful, and to reveal my life in all its variegated colors would be to commit an indiscretion against which the maturity of my years warns me.

But there are two phases of my life that I feel are worth recording because they touch on universal human notes. The first is embodied in my youthful sports and adventures, so far at variance with those of the present generation as to seem incredible through very contrast. My own sons could no more understand my youthful adventures than I can fully comprehend theirs - yet the irresistible urge to express the healthy (though as yet uncontrolled) spirits of youth has never changed except in form.

Looking back at my own youth, I wonder not at the severity of my father in his attitude toward the vehicles I employed to express my vitality, but rather I find myself made more broadminded in my own attitude through my later appreciation of his understanding and self-restraint. If these vehicles seem so reckless and reprehensible to me in my maturity, what must they have seemed to him!

Just what has changed the attitude of the Head of the House toward his children since my youth has been the subject of much discussion. My father's word was law. Today there is a more lenient attitude on the part of the father, and a distinct change is apparent in the discipline of youth, whether for better or worse is perhaps still to be determined. One day, when discussing the fundamental features of the strength and weakness of the United States, in the broadest sense, with Doctor Redlich, Professor of Comparative Law at Harvard, who had happened to be Minister of Finance in Austria at the crucial moment when Franz Josef was assassinated, and the Great War became launched, I was deeply impressed by his statement that the glaring, outstanding faults of American life were lack of discipline and lack of respect. I have since wondered whether these demoralizing characteristics of our government and society are not the direct result of the changed relation between fathers and children.

When my father told me to do anything, I was expected to obey without discussion or excuse. He had been brought up in that way by his father, whose dominating character was manifested in his business as in his family. My grandfather employed perhaps a thousand men in the construction of steam-boilers, locomotives, standpipes, etc. If an order of his was not promptly carried out, and the offender's excuse was that he had forgotten, the old gentleman's retort, which became a slogan in the family, was, "Only fools forget, and I'll have no fools around me."

My father's attitude was quite the same. I recollect that on one occasion, in Winter, when my request to stay out until nine o'clock had been granted, I arrived home a few minutes after nine. Knowing perfectly well that when Father said nine o'clock it was not to be two or three minutes after nine, I did not dare to enter the house. Instead, I went down to the carbarns, about half a mile from home, where the horsecars were housed, and climbed into one which was at the back of the building, thinking that this particular one would not be taken out before morning. The horse-cars in those winter days had their floors covered with straw, and offered not too bad a place in which to sleep, even though the barn was not heated.

I had crawled into the straw, and was sound asleep, when someone stepped on me. I was rudely awakened by being grabbed by the back of the neck and jerked to my feet by an irate horse-car driver. He was a big fellow, and gave me a thorough thrashing. This was about four o'clock in the morning, and I had to nurse my bruises in the vicinity of the house until I saw Father leave for business at his usual hour, exactly five minutes of seven. It was only then that I dared to go in. Of course Mother had been disturbed at my absence and was happy over my return; but the expected reprimand from Father, on his return that night, came with dire certainty.

SPEAKING of car barns and horse-cars, I am reminded of the great occasion when the first electric car was run in the United States. I was taken to Lynn by my father, where this event was to take place. This electric car had been built by Thompson and Houston, which concern was the foundation stone of the present General Electric Company. The building was situated on the corner of Western Avenue and another street, on which there were large board gates. A trolley wire had been run from the yard across Western Avenue and around the Lynn Common. The streets were crowded with thousands of eager people. The picture might be compared to an assembly expecting Lindbergh's arrival or some other great flying feat of the present time. At the appointed hour, these large gates were thrown open, and, while a band played some appropriate tune, the electric car came forth having on board the Governor, his staff, and other prominent people, made its trip around the Common, and returned to the yard without mishap. Thus a new era was born. It is impossible to describe the enthusiasm of the people.

Following this demonstration, Father became interested in the development of electric street-railways. In association with

E. P. Shaw and J. Ferguson, he secured the horse-car franchises in many districts of New England, especially Massachusetts, and changed these horse-cars over into electric-car companies. At the time the Massachusetts Street Railway consolidation took place, Father was the director or president of fourteen different roads, making up the combination. Apparently the endeavor was a very nerve-racking procedure, largely due to certain features in connection with legislation and financing, so much so that Mr. Ferguson went insane, and Father had to take his interests over, which I presume was quite a financial burden. Later Mr. Shaw became financially involved, and it fell upon Father to take over his interests also. All this Father accomplished, and thus reaped the financial benefits from the various enterprises. It is interesting to note in this connection how history repeats itself. My father was far-sighted in realizing that electric-cars must push the horse-car into the discard, but he could not possibly have foreseen how automobiles and busses would later place streetrailways in the same disadvantageous position.

An incident recalled by this comment on horse-cars was when my young friend Billy Robinson and I once visited my grandmother's house in Charlestown, and had been given the privilege of ransacking the garret and cellar, which portions of a house were then, as now, of special interest to a boy's curiosity. On this occasion we discovered a small, old-fashioned hand organ, which Grandmother said we could have. This we took away with us on a horse-car. On our way home to Chelsea I cranked the organ, much to the amusement of everybody on board, and Billy got up and gravely passed the hat. Strange as it may seem, we found willing givers. Some of the tunes were· familiar to many of the passengers and they joined in the chorus, thus making the trip an unusually jolly affair. We further amused the passengers by playing the tunes backward.

An adventure of quite a different character, on which my memory has been refreshed by Kate Casey, my Irish nurse of early childhood, who likes to reminisce, occurred when I was perhaps seven or eight years of age. At that time, my family was living about a mile from the Chelsea railroad station. With Charles Mitchell, who later became one of the outstanding figures in American finance, I set out on an undetermined journey, premeditated or not, I do not know.

We found ourselves at the railroad station, where we watched a train come in, headed for Boston. The engineer and the fireman left the engine cab to fix something near the cowcatcher. I cannot believe that we had heard about train robbers and such adventures as those of Jesse James, but Charlie and I stole aboard the engine and secreted ourselves in the coal tender. After the train got underway, I presume we became frightened. At all events, we crawled out of the coal and appeared in the engine cab, much to the astonishment of the engineer and the fireman. We were well cared for, and eventually, we arrived at the Boston & Maine Eastern Division Station, then located in Haymarket Square, Boston, and now the site of the Haymarket Relief Station. The engineer must have been a kindly soul, for he took us somewhere for lunch and then back to Chelsea with him in the engine-cab on his afternoon trip out.

While Charles and I were faring as few boys have ever done, our families were not so happy. The usual search being unsuccessful, the lunch hour past, and no report of us, my father was summoned from his office in Boston. He acted with his usual directness. As the police-force had been unsuccessful in locating us, he insisted that the fire-department be called out. Apparently prominent citizens could make quite an appeal in those days. I am told that the engineer wrote a note which he gave to me before he dropped us off at the Chelsea station, where we were captured by the firemen as we stood on the platform waving to our new friend who, in our opinion, was the greatest man we had ever met. We were returned home by our captors, and I am told that our greeting was not as pleasant as our departure from our new friend, the engineer. However, I rather gathered that we were welcome in spite of severe comments and a good licking. I believe from rumors that the engineer-friend received a reward and a reprimand at the same time.

Returning to the subject of parental discipline, if I had an appointment with my father at his office, which I sometimes did, he stated the hour at which I was to be there. I always made it a point to arrive at least several minutes before the appointed time. When he said one o'clock, he did not mean five minutes before or one minute past; he meant one o'clock, and I always saw to it that my watch was correct. I would stand outside the office-entrance until about one minute before the appointed hour, when I would go in. It should be said, on the other side, that if he had an appointment with me at one o'clock, he was ready to receive me at that hour.

There is little question that this sort of discipline and the accompanying respect inculcated are fundamental in the development of character. Just what has changed it is speculative; but certainly it has changed. The scientific age has applied itself to youthful sports as to everything else. Children are placed under the charge of instructors as soon as they are old enough to learn to swim, to skate, to play tennis, hockey, golf, or whatnot. This has increased the proficiency of youths in athletic sports, but I wonder if it hasn't taken some of the fun out of it to have even their pastimes included among their lessons.

My first recollection of sporting adventure was watching and collecting tadpoles in a small stream in Hamilton, Massachusetts. This brook, which ran through a meadow and pine grove, was of absorbing interest to me at that time - when I had attained perhaps the age of six or seven. This stream was my paradise. I thought about it after I went to bed. I often dreamed about it, and I stole away to it on every opportunity. The princes and princesses, the castles, and all the happy associations of my fairy stories were tangibly located. there. It was at this stream that Little Red Riding Hood met the wolf; it was likewise the home of Robin Hood and every other childish hero.

My visits here were frequent, more so than my Irish nurse, Kate Casey, wished. She soon learned that, when I had run away, this was the place where I would be found. I remember how she once surprised me by grabbing me by the seat of my trousers as I lay flat on my stomach near a bush, watching a small pickerel wag his fins in an eddy under the mossy bank. My observations of the tadpoles changing their appearance by the development of legs, and the other successive steps of their evolution into frogs, was a cause of wonderment which has never since been surpassed. My imagination as to what the frogs might change into was never satisfied, and my childish respect for them was unbounded.

I had occasionally seen a turtle, and wondered whether that might not represent the transformation of the frog, as the frog had been the apotheosis of the tadpole. Further observation led me to believe that the turtle must be something apart from this evolutionary process, because while I could not catch a frog, I began to get bold enough to attempt to capture a turtle. For some time my attempts failed, but I remember clearly when first I surprised a turtle asleep on a log near the bank, and was thus enabled to capture it in the shallow water as it attempted to make its escape. From this experience came a satisfaction and confidence in my ability that words cannot describe, and the punishment which I received for returning home with my clothes soaked through was a forgotten incident compared with the pleasure my successful adventure gave me.

During later years I have visited this brook from time to time, yet instinctively I always make my visits alone. Perhaps my boys would be sympathetic if they went with me, but they undoubtedly have little dreamlands of their own. If so, they would surely understand why I prefer to be alone.

GROWING UP
—A LITTLE

As a few years went by, not much had changed with the Old Farm Road gang. We had added a couple of new kids from the neighboring roads of Chestnut Street, High Street and Village Avenue. The Reed family had moved to Old Farm Rd when the Andresen family took what was considered a bold move and went to Duxbury, MA full time. Phil was the oldest, then Mimi and Sally. They had not moved too far; they had been just a couple of doors up on High Street. We would find all kinds of new activities with them right next door. So, our gang lost a few members and gained a few as well.

In today's world kids our age would have all sorts of organized sports options to keep them busy. We had only one option outside of school sports and that was for boys. Little league baseball was it. Whoever the coach was, it was his decision who made the team and who did not. A couple of boys tried and did not make it. So, we had to make our own sports and we got pretty creative about it.

We all had bicycles by that time. These were not very fancy bikes. No one had any gears. It was single speed, but they gave us some mobility. As long as we stayed on the sidewalks, we were allowed to ride to neighboring streets. Sometimes, we would ride over the Taylor's lawn at the cul-de-sac end of our road to Village Ave. This was also done in later years as a dare when first driving cars back in the old "hood" and we wanted to recreate what we had done earlier in life. Our world had expanded a lot with the two wheels, and we figured out all kinds of things to do with our bikes.

With this new mobility, some of the neighboring kids would ride over to Old Farm Rd and we would think up games to play on our bikes. After a little while we made up a game of bicycle polo. This was played with croquet mallets and tennis balls. It was quite a fun game and was great exercise as we peddled as hard as possible to get to the ball before the next guy. At some point, the players became too vested in winning at all costs. We got into riding the other guy off the ball and this inevitably led to some crashes, which also resulted in a bunch of skinned knees and maybe a trip to Dedham Medical or two.

Not to worry, it got worse. It was discovered that instead of riding someone off the ball, a mallet head stuck in the wheel spokes did an efficient job of stopping that bike. Unfortunately, if done on the front wheel, it also pitched some folks over the handlebars. We had no concept of wearing helmets. In fact, there were not any available. So, there were some more skinned knees and a few cut heads, resulting in more trips to Dedham Medical. On one occasion, Phil's sister Mimi was in on the game and a strong competitor. Roger Cheever from over on Village Ave was also participating. During a fast chase with Roger and Mimi, the mallet slipped out of Mimi's hand and lodged in Roger's front wheel. This wiped out a number of wheel spokes, caused some other bicycle damage and the subsequent crash skinned up Roger's knee or knees. He limped on home with his now badly damaged formerly brand-new bike.

Soon after, his father visited the Reed's house and demanded that Loring (known as Sport to his children) buy a new bicycle for his son. Sport could be fairly blunt, and he told Mr. Cheever that it was an accident and he had no intention of buying a new bike. When Mr. Cheever complained again, Sport told him maybe Roger shouldn't play with us, if he thought our games were dangerous and that none of us would intentionally hurt another kid. Then he calmly closed the door with Roger and his father standing there. After several of these crashes and emergency trips to the doctors, whatever family owned the croquet set took it back and locked it up. Bike polo was terminated.

That did not deter the idea of bike adventures. We had become a lot more adventurous in our riding and the distances we rode. Phil Reed had become fascinated by the Navy's Blue Angels and thought that we should try some of their maneuvers on our bikes. So tentatively at first, we tried a variety of crossing maneuvers in the turnaround area at the cul-de-sac of Old Farm Rd. We practiced this a lot and I do mean a lot, but we only had two bikes at the crossing area at a time due to a lack of room and also a lack of a grander vision. However, we were able to recruit a few new participants which made maneuvers a little more complicated requiring constant repetition. We also started what we called dog fights like military planes would do. We tied crepe streamers on the back fenders of our bikes and the object was to cut off the other guy's streamer with your front wheel. The person with the last streamer intact, was the winner. This was an offshoot of doing the same thing with our control line planes. More later.

A few miles away was an A & P grocery store. A & P was short for The Great Atlantic & Pacific Tea Company. As I remember, they were at the forefront of the big grocery chain stores. They had a large building and an even larger parking lot. There also were "Massachusetts blue laws" in those days. The blue laws required most larger businesses to be closed on Sundays. This was a combination of wanting folks to attend church on Sundays and also to give the workers a day off.

Whatever the reasons, we were glad that we could have the entire parking lot to our bike gang and here we practiced our more complicated Blue Angels maneuvers. The most difficult was like a four-leaf clover pattern. Each rider would make the outline of the cloverleaf and then head to the center. The objective was to time it so that each bike in succession crossed the center as close to the previous bike as possible. Timing was everything. At first we were quite far apart. Since it was new to us, it seemed like we were close. As we practiced every Sunday, we got closer and closer and increased the speed.

Then, on some Sundays, we would have more participants and we'd figure out how to include them into the maneuvers. This usually required slowing down the pace a little until the riders got the hang of it. On one such Sunday, we had some of the regular participants and once again, Roger Cheever. The regulars probably did not give him enough time to practice and understand just how important it was to hit dead center accurately. Our first major mishap was about to transpire.

Roger got t-boned at the center point by Clint Smith. Roger was stunned by this and his formerly new bike replacement, sustained damage. As I recall, Clint was fine and so was his bike. Roger may have suffered a concussion and some cuts. He was then standing by his bike in a daze.

So, to minimize any further damage, it was decided that we should turn the technical maneuvers into our dog fight tactics. We tied crepe streamers on the back of our bikes. Then we used the large area to see if we could cut off the streamer on everyone else's bike and eventually be the one person who still had a streamer. This required riders to try to catch up to other bikes and have an offensive strategy as well as a defensive strategy for the biker being chased. I don't exactly remember who was the chaser, Phil or Mimi. I do remember that after a bit, the person who was being chased (the "chasee") rode at a high speed directly toward poor Roger still standing there beside his bike. The chasee was vulnerable to being taken out of the game because they had the "chaser" right on their tail and their crepe paper streamer was getting nipped off slowly, but surely, by the chaser's front wheel running over it. In a classic move, to get the chaser off its tail, the chasee aimed right at Roger, sped up, and then swerved away from Roger at the very last instant. The chaser, of course, had their eyes down, looking only for the crepe paper streamer that was being chased and nipped off with their front tire from the back of the bike they were chasing. So, the chaser, looking down at the chasee's streamer, was not looking up at what was right ahead of the two bikes: poor dazed Roger, standing by his bike.

The chaser didn't see Roger until the chasee made the sudden swerve, but then it was too late, and the chaser T-boned Roger's bike again. Fortunately, Roger was standing on the opposite side of his bike from the contact point (dead center on the side of the bike), but he still took a huge hit himself. He was clearly dazed again, and his bike was not in good shape.

I don't recall how or if he was transported to Dedham Medical. It might have been someone trying to help, or it might have been that one of the gang rode their bike to the Cheever house and got Mr. Cheever to come pick up the pieces. Or we may have somehow escorted Roger back home. Needless to say, once again he was not a happy camper nor was his father. Roger recovered, but he declined to participate in any additional Blue Angel activities. In fact, any of our Old Farm Rd activities.

The original four riders of the Blue Angels bike team rode on subsequent Sundays, but not with the same enthusiasm we originally had. We came up with some less technical maneuvers, but they did not have the same thrill as the center cross with just inches to spare. While there were not any crashes of the t-boning magnitude, it was not without some mishaps. But we survived without long-term consequences.

Of the core group of riders, both Phil and I went on to get our pilot's license. I got my license while in college and came close to flying in the military, but made the decision that I did not want to spend the extra years required in service to do so. I regret that I did not as I likely would have flown helicopters and that is something that I still wish I had learned to do. Phil got his license in high school in Arizona and later became a very accomplished pilot. In 1990 he took a couple of years off to build a Glasair III aircraft.

The Glasair was like a small fighter with 320 knots top dive speed, stressed to 9 G's, and fully aerobatic. With that plane, he later went to a fighter combat school in Phoenix and got their "top gun" award classification for private pilots which is likely the highest honor that a civilian pilot can reach. And all that started in the A&P parking lot. He also went on to own Kitfox Aircraft which sold airplane kits.

Phil Reed in his Glasair.
The plane in which he earned his "top gun" award classification.

My father also earned his pilot's license while in college. Then he stopped flying until later in life. He became an active pilot again in his late 50's. He owned and flew several different planes all low wing tricycle gear. However, he learned in a high wing tail dragger. Two different styles of aircraft that required different techniques for take-off or landing. I went the other way. I learned in a low wing tricycle gear and moved to a high wing tricycle gear. Not that much of a change.

Then, in the '80s, my father decided to build his own plane. It took about 2 1/2 years and took over the cellar and the garage in their house in Dover. The plane was a Rutan design Quickie. Dick Rutan designed and flew the Voyager in the first non-stop flight around the earth. His plane design was radical because the horizontal stabilizer was on the nose just behind the engine. They are usually on the tail. This made the plane hard to stall. Shortly after my father's plane was finished it had to be certified by a test pilot, who came out to the plane which was at the Plymouth, MA airport. The pilot had front and back parachute packs. My father asked if he would bail out if the engine failed. The pilot said, "You bet. At the first sign of trouble, I'm out." All my father could see was 2 1/2 years of work disappearing. There was no trouble. Several years later the Smithsonian Air & Space Museum put out a notice that they wanted a Quickie donated to be displayed alongside the Voyager and the other Rutan designed plane which was a VariEze.

My father's plane was picked from a large number of entrants. I remember asking him if he was going to fly it down there. No, he indicated. His friend, Bob Greaves, and my father cut the fuselage in half and loaded the plane on a trailer. Once at the Air and Space Museum, they were given a work area and all the tools and supplies to put the plane back together. It should have taken a couple of days, but they took their time as my father wanted it to be perfect and most importantly, they had the ability to wander in the museum hangers at will.

Author's father built and donated this Rutan design Quickie to the National Air & Space Museum.

Once back home, he told me several times that one could not believe all the aircraft that are stored in the hangers. They saw a lot and sat in a few. His plane was on display next to the Voyager at the Air & Space Museum on the Mall in Washington, DC for a while. I had the privilege of seeing it there. Today, it is still on display at the Steven F. Udvar-Hazy Center of the museum in Chantilly, VA, near Dulles Airport. It was and still is a great honor.

Our bike riding was never considered to be pure exercise, although it was. The bicycle was a mode of transportation or a tool to be used for other games. Today it seems as though bikes are used mostly as a form of exercise first and as a mode of transportation second, although that too may be changing.

FINDING TROUBLE

It really wasn't that we were interested in causing trouble. It just seemed to easily find us. We had little concept that our escapades would be considered malicious behavior. We were just boys being boys in a different time. I'm not sure that we were different than a lot of boys our age. The major dissimilarity was that we had access, with or without permission, to a lot of the implements that played a major part in our mischief.

To some extent, guns have always held a fascination with boys. It was rare in my early years that girls had the same interest in guns. I cannot recall at what age it was, but just about every boy in the neighborhood had a BB gun which had a lever cocking action to propel the BB. One or maybe two had pump action guns and right or wrong it was always believed these were of superior fire power. These guns did not generally cause serious bodily harm unless one was hit in the eye and that really would cause damage. "Do not shoot at any people with this gun," was likely the first admonition from our all our collective parents. Of course, we nodded our heads in agreement. Oh, ya!

At first, we had shooting contests to see how many cans could be hit and how far away they could be hit. This evolved into trying to hit smaller and smaller objects. In general, the guns did not have great accuracy and it varied widely from gun to gun. When one of our group was able to consistently hit very small objects, the rest of us gave credit to the gun and rarely to the marksman. Not always true. Many years later, most of us watched a marksman who Phil Reed's father Loring Reed arranged to give a shooting demonstration to the skeet shooters of The Country Club and the Dedham Country & Polo Club. This marksman could consistently throw up a washer the size of a nickel and shoot a BB right through the middle. A piece of scotch tape across the hole, showed where the BB had gone. This made us a lot more respectful of the shooter's ability as well as the gun's.

We soon tired of plinking at cans, bottles and other inanimate objects and we turned our sights to hunting squirrels. More accurately to shooting in the squirrels' direction. Hiding near bird feeders became a big pass-time, waiting for a squirrel to show up. While most parents did not mind us attempting to bag a squirrel, they did mind if we shot any birds. So, we were careful not to. Occasionally, we had the opportunity to go to my maternal grandparents' farm in Dover. This was real country and in our imaginations filled with game for our mighty BB guns. My grandmother, Evie Soule, was happy to have us go after squirrels. In fact, she was way ahead of us. She liked to feed and watch the birds and was very annoyed when squirrels would take over the feeder and deplete it of seed for the birds. So, she had my grandfather build a large bird feeder which she kept full of seed. That, of course, attracted any number of squirrels. However, the feeder had two metal bars spaced about 10 inches apart. Too far for any birds to contact both at the same time. But they were just right for a squirrel to jump up to the first then reach forward toward the seed and contact the second bar. They only did that once; I can assure you. Each metal bar was wired to one side of a cutoff extension cord which was plugged into an electric outlet. When the squirrel contacted both it was zapped. That basically limited our shooting opportunity around the feeder, until my grandfather, Bill, got tired of replacing the old glass screw-in fuses used in those days, which would often short out when the squirrel got shocked. After that we had more shooting chances and everyone was happy. We also found the old farm dump where tin and glass targets were plentiful. So, we were kept occupied with shooting activities when in Dover.

But boys being boys, we eventually forgot the words of warning from our parents and decided to have some team warfare with our BB guns back in the neighborhood. No shooting above the neck. Ya, sure. During one particularly hot battle, there were a number of casualties. The event took place at the Reed's house on High Street, since they had a sizable yard and a bunch of outbuildings. The first man down was Gus Bartlett. He was shot by Phil Reed right between the eyes. It left a pretty good welt and Gus, even being one of the tougher kids in the crowd, ran for home with flowing tears. It was probably the shock as well as the pain. After a few days, he did not hold a grudge and was back for more action. I was the second casualty. I was sneaking along a picket fence with tightly spaced uprights. Just space enough for a BB. My shoulder was against the fence. Unseen by me, Phil was right next to the fence on the other side. He nailed me point blank just below my t-shirt sleeve. Well, BB's can penetrate, I found out. Before I could examine the damage, I was after Phil trying to smack him with the butt of my gun. He made for his back porch and into the house locking the door. The BB was stuck in my skin and visible, so a little squeezing got it out. The resultant wound gave me a very nice red badge of courage for a few days. I was pissed off at Phil for a little while as much as anything because he was laughing heartily as he ran to the house door. But, with a little time, we all got over it and moved on.

After a few years of playing with BB guns, we naturally looked at something with a little more power. Most all of our parents hunted and by this time some of us had been allowed to go hunting with them. So, we understood gun safety and the fact that something like a .22 caliber bullet could travel a long, long way and if it hit a person, it would be very, very bad. Our parents also had substantial gun collections, some way better than others. Most of these were kept in unlocked display cases. My father had only hunting shotguns. But Sandy Darrell's father, Dike, had an impressive and varied collection of rifles, shotguns and handguns.

They lived on the street that was next to and parallel to Old Farm Rd. So, his gun closet was a frequent place for inspection and subsequent planning about how and where to try some of them.

Sandy Darrell and Spider Andresen
in front of the authors childhood home at 7 Old farm Rd, Dedham, MA

I'm not exactly sure why, but Sandy and I decided that we needed to try some of the smaller handguns in .22 caliber. The Darrells had a big barn garage at the back of their property with a sizable loft. There were old hay bales in there, so we set them up at either end. Then we proceeded to be carefully dumb by shooting across the loft at the hay bales where the other guy was hiding behind. We at least did not shoot directly at the bales which we each hid behind. I guess that it gave you a different sensation by having the noise come at you instead of away. That was a one-time happening, and, luckily, we moved onward without any adverse damage. But yes, we were stupid enough to play cowboys will real guns.

For the next episode, Mr. Darrell was in his office which was close to the gun closet, but not directly visible to it. Sandy and I had plotted to get a pump action .22 rifle out of the closet and out of the house, so we could go down by the Charles River and see if we could shoot a muskrat.

The rifle easily came apart in two pieces. Sandy had the stock under his sweatshirt. I had the barrel assembly down my pant leg, which required a stiff legged walk. Assuming that we had been oh so clever, we were sauntering toward the front door. Mr. Darrell barely looked up and said, "Don't shoot anybody." We muttered something brilliant like, "Ahhh, ok!." We never figured out if we had actually been caught or if that was just Mr. Darrell making a light-hearted statement. In any case, we didn't shoot much of anything and even got the gun back, safe and sound. Part of the excitement was just the planning of how to accomplish our goal and then putting the plan in action.

However, not shooting anyone was a close call on another totally inadvertent episode. After our live ammo craziness in the garage barn, we took up practicing our bow and arrow skills. We had an early recurve bow and to be honest, I am not sure where it came from. We set up a straw filled target on the fence at the back of the Darrell's yard. That fence was the dividing line between the Archibald's house on Old Farm Rd and the Darrell's on Village Ave. All went well for a number of sessions as we got used to hitting the target with heavy tipped target arrows. We kept backing away to see if we could still be accurate by putting a little bit of an arc in the arrows flight, which required aiming high. One day, we decided to get a hunting arrow with a sharp crossed blade on it. What we did not understand was that the hunting arrow was much lighter in the tip than the target arrow and it had better flight dynamics. Having tried to put this out of my mind, I am not sure if Sandy or I fired the arrow. It was aimed as if it needed the same arc as the target arrow at a long distance. It did not. So, it sailed over the six foot high fence. All we heard was the breaking of glass and we knew that it was time to make ourselves very scarce. We dumped the bow behind a bush near the Darrell's house and headed up Chestnut Street toward High Street and the safety of my family's backyard. What we did not know until later was that the arrow went through a closed window into the kitchen and stuck in a cabinet under the counter. Mrs. Archibald was walking into the kitchen at that very time and thought that someone was trying to shoot her. Since no one had seen us, we feigned no knowledge and said that we had left the bow and arrows on the ground near the target and some other person must have shot our only brand-new hunting arrow. We must have looked sorry that this happened, and we were, because we even got the arrow back. I believe we promptly lost it down near the river on another outing to get a muskrat. Mrs. Archibald was prone to hyperbole and told all the neighbors how someone had tried to shoot her in her own kitchen. She was known as "For Christ's sake Priscilla." That was because every time she came up with something like this, her husband, Fred, would exclaim, "Oh, for Christ's sake Priscilla!"

We learned that backyards were too small for target practice of any kind, but it did not mean that we lost interest in anything that went "bang!" In fact, our continued fascination with all things explosive had been there for years and remained there for a long time after.

A LITTLE MORE TROUBLE

I have said this before, and it is a generalization. Generalizations can usually be proven wrong. Boys like things that go bang or cause an explosion. At least, in my youth they did. In most cases, it was an inherent interest which was bolstered by youthful experience and access to some of those things that could explode.

As mentioned earlier, my father drove down and up the East Coast as a salesman. On his travels, he passed through a lot of states where fireworks were legal. They were not in Massachusetts or Maine in those days. He never failed to come home without an assortment of fireworks. The ones that over time caught our interest the most were the cherry bombs and ashcans, also called M-80s. These were not the same as what is available today. If one of these went off in your hand, it would likely take some of your hand with it. The noise was startling, and they had the added benefit of being able to explode in or under water. Once the fuse was lit, it stayed lit until the firecracker exploded. It is likely that the sheer power of these firecrackers was the basis for having the federal government declare them outlawed in 1966.

One year, while we were at the Wareham summer house, we drove over to the Kittansett Club in Marion to watch the Fourth of July fireworks. My guess is that I was eight or nine. My father had a Pontiac Bonneville convertible, and we were traveling with the top down. He also had a supply of cherry bombs. As we drove down Point Road leading up to the Club, I was sitting in the front seat. He told me to push in the cigarette lighter. Of course, I did. When it popped, meaning it was glowing hot, he told me to pull it out and turn it toward him. I did and with his left hand he lit a cherry bomb and dropped it outside the car onto the road. As it got close to the car behind, it exploded. My mother in the back seat was not pleased, but the game was on. The car behind watched for the drop then swerved to keep from running over it. Dad did it a few times more pretending to be a Navy ship depth charging an enemy submarine. When we got to the Club. He continued to set off some of the cherry bombs. It was Fourth of July after all. Two policemen came over and nicely informed my father that fireworks were illegal in Massachusetts. My father nodded politely in agreement, but as soon as they had turned to walk away, he rolled a lit cherry bomb in their direction. He was sheepishly walking away as the firecracker exploded and they jumped around, hands close to their sidearms. They just shook their heads in somewhat amused disgust. Today, anything close to that would require jail time and fines. It was most certainly very different than today. It was also, right or wrong, one of the many introductions to playing with things that exploded. The fact that our fathers also did this was a tacit acknowledgement that it was okay.

    Early on, we discovered that we could build makeshift pipe cannons to play with. These were made with aluminum tubing crimped at one end and with a hole drilled near that end. It you took a fuse from any old firecracker and inserted it in the hole, then take God knows how many paper safety match heads and pack them into the bottom of pipe around the fuse. Put in something as a wad to keep the compression and then maybe some small stones as projectiles and a little more wadding. These kinds of cannons would make a little sort of explosion and send out a scatter of projectiles. We thought it was pretty neat and were obsessed with them for a while. I remain surprised there were any paper matches left anywhere around the neighborhood or the town for that matter, because we used one heck of a lot of them. Then one day a new participant joined us in the Estabrook's back yard where they had a garden shed that was somewhat out of sight and therefore a good place to pack and fire our cannons. Tim Norris was the newbie, and he lived a little ways off in Westwood. Since he was new to this activity and he likely wanted to make an impression, I would guess that he got overly excited about packing down the match heads. He did it so hard that they inadvertently exploded. Although never confirmed, the suspicion was that he had used at least some of the strike anywhere variety of matches. That was a real no-no! Unfortunately, his hand was over the closed end of the pipe which blew apart. His hand was badly hurt. So, he was taken by a nearby parent to Dedham Medical. He recovered ok, but it took a while. Our little cannon escapade was shut down and we began to think about how we might use some of the fireworks that were also available, surreptitiously at least.

Another brief adventure took place in the Estabrook's back yard. As mentioned earlier, the shed where the cannon incident happened was out of sight because it was down in a fairly wide gully. At the edge of the lawn were some substantial trees. Lower down across the gully were some other trees. So, someone came up with the idea of putting a long rope across the gully and making what essentially would be a zip line. I do not recall our calling this by that name. It was just going to be a heck of a ride across the gully. I'm not sure what we used to suspend from the rope. Likely it was a pulley with a hook and was part of the whole block and tackle arrangement that made up the zip line. Again, I'm not sure how many times this ride was used, but Ricky Estabrook was zipping across the gully and the zip line failed. He crashed to the ground and luckily only suffered some abrasions and a bruised ego. The zip line was terminated. Onward.

One of the great things about those early cherry bombs and ashcans beyond their explosive capacity was that the fuse would work under water. So, we began to experiment with ways to weight them down and have them explode underwater. This dampened the noise but made an impressive water explosion if done in shallow water and a major ka-whump when submerged in deeper water along with an impressive shock wave and foaming hump in the water. If there happened to be a fish in the vicinity, it was usually toast. We found that a wrap of plain old solder wire did the trick for shallows and a number of wraps for greater depth. Luckily we were not stupid (I didn't use dumb on purpose) enough to ignite and allow to explode a solder wrapped ashcan out of the water. It would have acted like a hand grenade, sending shrapnel in every direction.

Somewhere around this time, another new kid, Clint Smith, arrived in the neighborhood. His family lived on Village Ave almost across from the end of Old Farm Rd, so he could ride his bike across the Taylor's lawn and join in the activities. I cannot remember if I was trying to impress him with my "expertise" in all thing's fireworks. However, I had a bunch of the large Chinese firecrackers that made more of a paper mess than an explosion. They had a finer powder in them then did the cherry bombs or ashcans, which had a granular "flash powder." We did not understand the difference in the powder types but could easily see it. We tended to fool around with the firecracker powder since they did not have the impressive bang and therefore were expendable for other uses. We had removed the powder from a bunch of the large firecrackers and had made a line of powder leading up to a larger pile at the end along the top flat rail of our yard fence. I am not sure what Clint was doing with one hand near the larger pile, but it was there as the end of the long line of powder was lit. We had thought that it would be a long sizzle and then a big poof. What occurred was an almost instantaneous ignition. Clint's hand was badly burned. I had no idea what I was doing, but I tried to help by bandaging it. Clint went home and his visiting Aunt Shirley, who was a nurse, removed my medical handiwork and did things correctly. Later she told me that the skin on his whole hand could almost be removed like a glove. Lesson learned the hard way, again.

Clint Smith (L) and the author
in front of the Archibald house on Old Farm Rd.

A few years later, Clint would also be the target of one more explosive event. Clint was diagnosed with some sort of illness that was considered to be highly contagious as his friends from Old Farm Road were not allowed to go into their house. We visited through a kitchen window in the back of the house. On one visit, Clint was occupying his convalescence by making a cake. We watched as he slathered the chocolate frosting all over the cake and then placed the finished product in the nearby breadbox. We said our goodbyes and pretended to leave, but we hid by the garage for a short while. I believe that Phil Reed was with me on this visit. One of us had a firecracker of some sort and our plan was to sneak back, get into the house and blow up the cake. Clint heard the explosion and rushed into the kitchen to find his baking efforts stuck to the walls and the ceiling and the breadbox was blown apart. We were nowhere to be found and made it our business to stay away from Village Avenue until things simmered down. Both Clint and his father, Traver, commented on this event for years.

Thinking back to our summer trips to Wareham, my grandfather, Dr. John H. Cunningham, had a 1-gauge cannon that had brass reusable shell casings. It made an impressive noise but was rarely used which was a real disappointment. Somehow one of these empty shell casings had made its way onto my father's workbench in the cellar. There it resided for quite a while, until Bob Mann and I decided to see if we could make a very large explosion using the components from a number of cherry bombs. It is hard to recall how many cherry bombs were carefully cut open, but enough to fill the brass casing between 1/3 and 1/2 full. Prior to putting in the powder, the expired detonation cap was punched out from the inside. The resultant hole was just big enough for a cherry bomb fuse. That was stupid mistake number one. If you want to make a big bang, get a long fuse so you can get the heck away from the explosive device after lighting the fuse. But that was all we had, and we tried to keep as much outside as possible. Once the powder was in, we set the casing open end up with the fuse down between the two sides of the vise on the workbench. We took some wadding, likely just some crumpled newspaper and put that in. Then a 50 cent piece was inserted. This was just about a perfect fit. We gingerly compressed this and were able to punch 4 holes at 90 degrees around the casing. Nails were inserted and peened over to keep the wadding and 50 cent piece firmly in place. The end of the shell casing was then squeezed flat with the vice. Voila!!! We had made a very large firecracker. Stupid mistake number 2 was that what we had crafted was a lot closer to a hand grenade than a firecracker. It is easy to see now, but we were oblivious to that then. We inherently did not want to be near this when it exploded but that was more for what we expected the noise would be than the danger of flying shrapnel. Now the question was what do we do with it?

I don't believe that we ran right out and torched it off. My recollection is that we hid it away for a day or two while we tried to figure out the best place to fire it off. I do know that it was early Winter as we were not out late, and it was fully dark and chilly on the evening of this adventure. We wandered down to the end of Old Farm Rd and over the end to Village Ave. We walked down the street away from town and away from the Norfolk County jail, which was three blocks toward the village. There were some streetlights in those days, but they were few and far between. We ended up in front of Clint Smith's family's house. They were away as no lights were on. No one was out on the sidewalk as far as we could see in either direction. Along the sidewalk there was about a 4 foot high stone retaining wall. The explosive device fit nicely in-between a couple of the rocks. We looked at each other and decided that this was as good a place as any. Dumb idea number three. We should have simply gone off into the woods somewhere. But we lit the fuse and ran like heck back toward the end of Old Farm Rd. We were a good distance away when it detonated, and the concussion still almost knocked us over. We knew that we had to pick up the pace of our exit. We ran right by the Mann's house and up to the end of the road by my family's house. We then slowed down and tried to look innocent. As far as we knew we had not been seen by anyone during our escape. All we knew was that the explosion was far bigger than we ever imagined. We made a pledge to each other to never mention this to anyone.

What would be a major response to an explosion of this kind today, in retrospect was amazingly non-existent. At least, we were never aware of much of anything. Several days later, we got up the courage to ride our bikes over the end of Old Farm Rd and onto Village Avenue. As we rode by the scene of the explosion, there were still some rocks from the wall on the sidewalk. Not a shred of evidence of the shell casing. That was probably good. And later we learned that a couple of windows in the house opposite the wall were cracked. Ok, we decided that we had learned we could make a big bang, but there were consequences. On to the next event.

While we never really lost our interest in explosives, we tried to use our experiences a little more productively. Phil Reed and I discovered that one could buy model jet engines that ran on a solid fuel, all available by mail order. So, we started to play around with these. At first, we just secured them to model cars and sent them hurtling down the road, usually to disastrous results. We even tried to attach them to large (for us at that time) gliders. That was also unproductive as we did not have any very large open space readily available for this effort. Then we got the brilliant idea of using them for what they were designed for. Propelling rockets skyward. And that was the direction where we had the most space. Truly, the sky was the limit. So, we played with the rockets until we got them to go high enough that they were mere specs in the sky. The real trick was to find the rockets after they returned to earth. Usually, they were in the Walkers very ample backyard which was behind the Reeds back fence. Over a matter of months, we got better and better results until one day the rocket simply disappeared. We never really looked for it as we had no idea where it went. No neighbors ever made any complaint about finding the remains on their property.

We were undeterred, we went for bigger and better. At that time, Phil's father, Loring, who was happy with our soda selling abilities, was working at the Reece Corporation in Waltham.

It was a family business that had invented and manufactured sewing machines which could sew buttonholes for clothing manufacturers and eventually also pockets. Well, they had an extensive machine shop capability. So, Phil designed a jet engine which would slide into an aluminum tube for the rocket body and a nose cone was crafted for the front end. These were beautifully machined pieces made of aluminum bar stock that were made in the Reece Corporation machine shop. As we began to once again get the rocket to go higher, we ran into the problem of losing parts. We kept having to go back to the well for replacement parts when things disappeared. Finally, Phil designed a way to have the nose cone come open after the rocket reached its zenith and a parachute would deploy to slow the descent and to allow us to track it to its landing point for retrieval. We kept refining things until once again the rocket totally disappeared in the sky. Thank God, there were not many planes flying in the area, as it seemed likely that we were high enough to interfere with a transiting plane. The last rocket was just that. We had worn out our welcome and good will with the Reece Corp. We went back to the smaller purchased rockets, but they had lost our interest.

Our next direction was with gas engine model airplanes with control lines. While I am sure that radio-controlled airplanes existed then, we did not have the means to buy them. The control line models could be built and flown for pretty reasonable prices. They were also easy to learn to fly, although it did take some repetition to get used to things like learning to remember instinctively how to unwind the control lines when you did loops. Also, when you flew upside down the up and down controls, which were all you had, were backwards. A few mishaps later, we got better at flying and good at repairing damaged planes. Toward the end of our enthusiasm about control line flying, we would put a 3 ft long piece of crepe paper streamer on the tail of two planes and have aerial dogfights to see who could cut the tail off the other plane. Like some of our other adventures we began to move in other directions and the planes got shelved and used less and less frequently.

We never did get into radio-controlled planes then, as mentioned, likely due to the cost and secondarily due to the lack of necessary area. Much later in my life, my father, Mac Cunningham, built a radio control model of the plane he learned to fly in. It was the Piper J-3, which was a tail dragger style of landing gear meaning the plane would sit nose up until it gained enough speed to raise the tail and subsequently take off. He had done a beautiful job making this plane and when it was ready he taxied it around on the driveway in front of the Dover house. One day in the fall of the late '60s, he said "Let's go up to the polo field at the Dedham Club and fly it." My response was "Ok, let's go!"

After arrival at the field, Dad looked at me and said, "You fly it! You have your pilot's license." I was dumb enough to think that I could translate my experience to radio control. I taxied the plane around for a little and pointed it down the field. I pushed the throttle forward and as the tail came up off the ground, my father announced that the up and down aileron controls were backwards. I should have immediately pulled back on the throttle and simply taxied the plane back to us. I did not.

In my head, I thought that I could handle the reversal. I did for the takeoff. I turned the plane to come back around the field and had not realized that there was a strong crosswind pushing the plane out toward the trees on the side. In fact, the plane had gone over the trees and I wanted to get it up above the trees again. I panicked and pulled back on the up and down stick, which sent the plane into a power dive. I did not recover from that mistake. The plane buried nose first into the ground about five feet off the 18th green. The plane was a total loss. The only good thing was not having to pay to repair the green. I have always wanted to fly radio control planes but have been haunted by my complete destruction of many hours of my father's work. He seemed okay with it, but inside I am sure he was very disappointed. He built another not to fly, a model Quickie, like the real one he also built.

Back to the earlier years, there would be other adventures with models that we crafted.

Author in the cockpit of a Piper Cherokee, where he learned to fly.

11
PLAIN DEVILTRY

JOHN H CUNNINGHAM

*D*eviltry in the present generation seems to be on the wane, which is probably a good thing. As schoolwork is much more exacting than during my youthful days, boys now have less time to themselves outside. Such hours as they might use to get together and carry out natural impulses of original nature are now occupied with organized sport lessons in skating, tennis, hockey, swimming, and everything else which used to be initiated by the boys themselves. The athletic advantages offered today are also quite different from our day. We had no baseball parks, hockey-rinks, swimming pools, automobiles, or movies. We had to create our own fun, and the most productive of all fun-factories were the "clubs" where some member could always be relied upon to think out some deviltry the other members had overlooked!

The nearest present-day approach to the "clubs" of my boyhood are the summer-camps, but modernm organization of these has destroyed the initiative, and the keen delight we took in the secrecy of our "doings" is completely eliminated by the supervision of counselors. Far be it from me, however, to deny that these losses to the boys are offset by fewer sleepless nights on the part of parents and the community!

Our first attempt at a club was made in the yard at the rear of my father's house on Shurtleff Street, in Chelsea, Massachusetts. The yard backed up against a church. A heavy, grapevine trellis had been built about ten feet from the pulpit-end of the church, to break the bareness of the wooden wall. This opening offered an inviting place to locate a camp, especially as one side was already supplied by the end of the church, and the grapevine trellis provided a structure on which to build another. In our architectural plans we figured that if we could nail a joist onto the wall of the church it would serve, with the grapevine trellis, as a suitable means of supporting a roof. With the plan decided upon, it only remained to secure our materials. The joist was acquired, after dark, and the few necessary spikes came from a bit of railroad construction which was going on not too far from the scene of our operations.

Everything progressed satisfactorily until directly after the following Sunday-morning service. The minister called on Father and confided that, when he had sat down in his chair, in back of the pulpit, he had caught his robes on a spike which somehow had been driven through the wall and into the back of his chair. An inspection of our activities supplied the necessary explanation, and our enterprise was summarily abandoned.

Our first club that actually came into existence was located under the piazza of a house at the corner of Washington Avenue and Carter Street, in Chelsea, into which my family had moved after my grandfather's death. Its approach was from beneath the back-door steps over a built-in box, containing the garbage barrel. By getting up onto this box, an opening which led under the piazza served as a passageway through which we could wiggle on our bellies for about twenty or thirty feet, and thus gain entrance to a rather large space underneath the piazza. There was not height enough to stand, but it was certainly secluded!

Here we collected the spoils of our adventures - all kinds of junk that we had picked up here and there, with quite an arsenal of small arms, mostly single-shot pistols ("Derringers"), wooden guns with grooves on the tops, through which round stones could be propelled by a heavy, round, cloth-covered elastic, attached to a wooden block, drawn back and caught by a hook. Released by a trigger, this made quite a gun, with which we killed birds - mostly sparrows, robins, chickadees, flickers, and occasionally pigeons. Most of these birds, with the exception of the chickadees, flickers, and robins, were stalked in the street, as they fed on the horse-manure. The other birds could only be secured by making expeditions into the nearby woods, which became important events. Our guns were real weapons, tabooed by our parents and therefore carefully secreted in our clubroom. Ammunition for the pistols and Flobert rifles, that we saved up to purchase, was hard to get, and, when acquired (usually from our parents' carefully secreted store), was skillfully concealed. A real expedition into the wilderness had to be undertaken before these pistols could be fired without danger of discovery.

We accumulated an abundance of literature in this clubroom—mostly Nick Carter's detective stories, which we used to "swipe" from nearby stores. This led to a call on the part of "Our Gang" for loose blouses, each with a heavy elastic around the waist. It was a garment that permitted the secretion of stolen objects, mostly Nick Carters or "Golden Days."

Our thieving adventures were well-planned, and always well-executed. We usually worked in pairs, comparative success defining leadership. The procedure was for two of us to enter the store, and while one "bad boy" requested something rarely called for, which we knew would not be easily attainable, the other boy would be innocently scanning the literature. At an opportune moment, he would surreptitiously slip one or more desired pamphlets into the loose blouse. I must admit that even our consciences were sometimes strained, but the joint responsibility in crime cemented us together in a way that less reprehensible misdemeanors could never have accomplished.

This club consisted of four members, and, as usual in most groups of boys, one of them was made the "goat." Our goat, Frank Slade, lived amid more luxurious surroundings at home than the rest of us. His father, a member of the old D. & L. Slade Spice Company, was rather a dude sportsman, and, fortunately for us, owned much gunning paraphernalia that we coveted. So it happened that many things we noticed while playing about the Slade house were earmarked to be taken to the club. Thus, we became stocked mostly by loot supplied generously but unwittingly by Frank's father.

On one memorable occasion a great adventure was undertaken. Frank "borrowed" from his father a double-barreled, 1 2-gauge shotgun and some cartridges. This gun, manufactured by Shaffer, the gunsmith on Elm Street, was one of the most expensive made. The breach-block and lock-plates were inlaid with gold designs of birds, and there was a gold plate in the stock with the owner's name engraved on it. It was the possession most treasured by Father Slade. Just why the boy took this particular gun instead of one of the many others he never explained. After a meeting of the club, we ventured forth, each secreting some part of the gun under his coat. Frank, being the goat, had to carry the barrel stuck down one of his trouser legs and stocking. (We were all still in short trousers.)

Frank Harris had won the privilege of shooting first by drawing the lucky straw. This made him the chief. He directed us to the "canyon," a small quarry about half a mile away. The "chief," with our assistance, finally succeeded in putting the gun together and loaded it. An old, empty, blasting powder can was put up as target, and Harris took his position among the rocks to demonstrate his prowess. Of course, like the rest of us, he knew all about shooting!

Unfortunately, however, he placed the stock of the gun under his arm instead of against his shoulder, and then pulled both triggers at once. With the explosion, the gun flew back, and the lever which is used to open the gun caught Frank in the cheek, tearing a long, deep gash. Harris fell back on the ground without a sound, and the gun flew through the air, landing among the rocks. The victim, when he came to, insisted that he had been shot.

The catastrophe was a matter of deep concern. We were fearful that Frank was going to die; but, apprehensive of the consequences of our misadventure and the possible seriousness of the situation, we were reluctant to go for help. We were a scared bunch of boys, and suddenly came to a realization that we were not as smart as we had thought ourselves.

When we recovered the gun, we found that the stock had been broken at the pistol-grip, and the barrels were badly dented and scratched. Harris, now an important banker, still wears the scar on his right cheek. It has graced many an important bank board meeting or financial conference. It is a matter of rather grim interest that this gun was repaired, and some years later was used by Frank Slade's father to blow off his head by placing the muzzle in his mouth and pulling the trigger with his toes.

After this shotgun episode we confined ourselves for some time to the wooden, elastic propelling-gun and slingshot. Slingshots were our most commonly used weapons. In the Fall we would go into the woods and get "Y" shaped branches of different sizes out of which to make them. The smaller ones were fitted with a few elastic strands to a small piece of leather, in which pebbles, BB or buckshot, were used as missiles. The leather of these slings often came from discarded gloves or shoes, but frequently gloves or shoes in fairly good condition used to disappear mysteriously, thus causing some family enquiry. The club had a great assortment of slings, and the excellence of their construction as well as the ability to use them were marks of distinction.

EXCURSIONS into the woods in the hunting-season were always events of competitive skill, and to wound or kill a flicker or chickadee (the most common game) gave additional standing to the successful nimrod. These spoils were the immediate explanation of the disappearance of absorbent cotton, thread, and hairpins from our mothers' work-baskets. Taxidermy, if it could be called that, occupied many of our secret hours, and on the rudely constructed shelves in the clubroom our handiwork was proudly placed on exhibition. Cats did not escape us, and we were early "salt-tanners." Our first coney rabbit, acquired with a slingshot, was a great triumph. After our skins were tanned, we attempted to make caps and gloves in real Indian fashion. Some of them were most original and amusing in appearance.

INTEREST in explosives, although suspended for a while after our shotgun experience, did not remain permanently latent. Gradually we again ventured into the quarry, and by stealth we "acquired" some metal caps from the blasting-shed where we had often watched the workmen attach them to explode the dynamite. We knew that by dropping a rock on them they would go off with a big "bang." These caps, which resembled somewhat a 38-caliber rifle-cartridge, were real prizes. Our amusement with them was to set one on a rock and place another rock on top of it. Then, dropping a heavy stone onto this set-up, an explosion with a loud report resulted. This same game was played with our pistol-cartridges after removing the bullets and replacing them with candle-wax or chewing-gum.

All this created a desire for greater events, and one day we not only took the fuse caps but also six sticks of dynamite. This promised real fun! After many conferences, the four members of the club started forth down a road that led into seclusion. Trepidation began to grow, and when we had gone about two hundred yards beyond the last house, which happened to belong to the mayor of the city, and which was built about a half-mile from the next nearest house, Frank Slade, our goat, got cold feet and deserted us. Harris, perhaps recalling his shot gun experience, sneaked away with him, leaving to Billy Robinson and me the opportunity of becoming greater heroes. Before leaving, they dropped their sticks of dynamite, which Billy and I picked up and put in our pockets, each then having three sticks and many caps.

That the desertion of our companions gave us apprehension we, of course, would not admit. As they lingered near the mayor's house, watching us, we decided that the big event should be carried out where they could observe it, and thus be humiliated that they had not stayed with us. We decided that the middle of the road, where we were, was just the place to pull off the explosion. We stuck several caps into one of the sticks of dynamite, and, finding a flat, hard spot in the road, placed a rock as large as a bucket on the top of our prepared charge. Billy was to set it off. After he bounced a good-sized boulder on our setup without results, I took a try.

I must have been successful. All I remember is raising the boulder above my head and throwing it with all my force, with the intention of turning away quickly as it left my hands. When I became conscious, I was in an apple-orchard about twenty yards from a fence and on a side hill, so that any view of the road was obscured. Nearby was Billy, groaning. We had been blown over the fence and had been given a ride of twenty-five or thirty yards. Things were pretty misty, and nobody seemed to come to our aid. When Billy and I collected our wits, it became apparent that we did not have on as many clothes as usual, and one of my shoes was missing. Billy was a sight, all bloody and terribly frightened. I found that I still had my three sticks of dynamite in my pocket, and Bill had both of his. These we buried in the ground, and then crawled to a small brook, not far away. Sitting in it, we noticed that the still water was getting red. This caused us much concern, and we agreed that we must be in a very bad way.

When we were able, we decided to go to my house, which was nearer than the Robinsons', and find out how badly we were hurt. Billy sat on the back-door steps, where he was to wait until I found out if we were seriously injured. Mother was in her sitting-room, knitting. As she observed my entrance, she let out a scream and fainted. My worst fears were confirmed. I went back to Billy and told him how Mother had passed out, so we must be really badly injured. He followed me back into the house, and between us we dripped considerable blood on the hall- and library floors. There were few telephones in those days, and we did not have one; but someone was sent for a doctor. When he came, he put each of us into the family bathtub, one after the other, and lathered us with soap, which stung plenty. Our bodies were covered with irregular punctures and small lacerations. Our faces were the only part apparently uninjured. Fortunately, we had turned our heads away before the explosion took place and showered us with the small bits of flying stone. I still recollect the Doctor picking pieces of stone out of my back and legs, and some of the scars still remain.

Billy and I remained in bed for many days, sleeping on our stomachs as our backs were altogether too painful to lie upon. We were the objects of much discussion in our families, and we received our full share of parental comment. Father had quite a bill for repairing the road, which was so damaged that it had to be closed to travel. The mayor's house had only a few windowpanes left in one side. The adventure certainly failed to increase our popularity in the neighborhood. Our deserting companions did not visit us during our confinement, but later we learned a lot about the event from them which Billy and I had overlooked. They both thought, when we went up in the cloud of dust, that the dynamite we had in our pockets had exploded. Why it did not is just one of those miracles.

THIS dynamite episode made somewhat of a breach in the relationship of the Gang for a long time. Our two deserters were self-conscious, and, as Billy and I recovered, they felt very much out of this most unusual picture. Family restraint was properly imposed, for a while at least, and we walked dismally around the piazza which covered our club-house without daring to enter, for fear we might be discovered and be taken to account for the various things we had secreted there. We knew very well that none of the grown-ups could possibly get through the narrow approach, but we did not dare to take a chance of having the clubroom discovered, as we knew that the family would make us clean it up and would forbid us to use it as a retreat. It was a long time before we ventured to re-establish ourselves, and then with great caution.

We had stored there some cigars and champagne from my father's wine-cellar which we were anxious to dispose of. This we finally removed and ingratiated ourselves with the street-cleaners by presenting them with several bottles. One old Irishman was in such a hurry to get a bottle open that he knocked the neck off by hitting it against the curbstone. For some time afterwards the street-cleaners seemed to be more numerous around our district, and, as we had dispensed all our generosity at once, we had to keep out of the way.

There was one old fellow who did not seem to do any work except in front of our house. Whether he felt that he had not received his full share of our generosity, or whether he had received so much that he was over-appreciative, I do not know; but he intimated that unless we again became good little fairies he would tell our fathers that we were young devils and bore watching.

This required the careful consideration of the Gang, which resulted in an unsuccessful attempt, not well planned, to yield to his blackmail. Father Slade's wine-cellar was used to store selected fruits as well as wines. There was a small window entering it from beneath the kitchen. Frank had managed to unlock this window in preparation for our raid, and one afternoon Billy Robinson and I set out to take up the new collection. We had carefully gotten through the window and gathered the bottles that we desired. I had crawled out, and Billy was handing the bottles up to me through the window when the cook surprised us, entering the wine-closet from the cellar. Billy made a rush for the window, but, unfortunately, put his foot on a watermelon as a step towards gaining access to the sill above. His foot went well into the melon, which he could not shake free. As he was on his stomach, trying to wiggle out of the window, the cook grabbed the watermelon, pulling it away and getting one of his shoes with it. Billy, minus one shoe, and I leaving the champagne where I had piled it, made our escape, but not without being recognized. We lost the use of a horse and carriage, a Saturday privilege, as punishment. The street-cleaner lost his anticipated pleasure; but for some reason he did not carry out his threat to denounce us to our parents.

This old fellow became quite a nuisance to us and occupied our attention considerably. He became such a pest that we felt we must do something about it. Just outside a high, thick hedge, which bordered the sidewalk in front of our stable, there was a sewer manhole. One day, as the old man was idly hanging about, pretending to sweep, and working towards this manhole, we conceived the idea of leading a hose from a growth of bushes in which we could be secluded, out through the hedge, so that one end of the hose would be in the hedge opposite the manhole. Having carefully secreted ourselves, we waited until our victim had moved down opposite. In the most distressed tone, we began to yell "Help" into the end of the hose which was nearest us. The sound coming from the other end in muffled tones, attracted his attention. Watching him as best we could, we would shout "Help" at proper intervals, and make other, varying sounds, announcing that we were in the sewer.

The old man became quite excited, and tried vainly to lift the cover. We were delighted to see him lean forward and shout down through the cover that he could not get the top off himself, but that he would go for help. We implored him not to leave us, but he ran to the fire-alarm box and pulled in the alarm. The whole fire-department arrived, and the cover was removed. The hose, by this time, was back in the stable, and we were up in the loft, enjoying the activities.

※

ONE of our favorite games was "tick-tack," a game which boys of the present time seem to know nothing about. It furnished a great deal of amusement when we were permitted to go out after dark. The game consisted of taking a long line, such as a fishline or kite-string, and tying a fishhook or a bent pin on one end. At a distance of about one foot behind the pin were attached one or more nails. The hook was inserted high on the window-frame, and, after being hidden, the jerking of the line made the nails bang against the window-pane. We always selected as our victims people who were not sympathetic with boys' pranks, and we got a good many chasings as a result. We usually pulled the line away when we started to make our escape, but on some occasions the string broke and we lost part of our gear. Another favorite pastime was what we termed the "shingle game." To carry this out to best advantage it was necessary to find a flight of steps which ran directly to the front-door. A shingle would be placed under the door, and on it would be piled rocks or tin-cans filled with rocks. The door-bell would then be rung. When the door was opened the shingle would drop out, and the tin-cans or rocks would go bumping down the steps. This game and tick-tack were our usual evening recreations if we had on hand nothing more exciting.

NEEDLESS to say, we led the police on the evening beat on many chases. While it happened that each of the four members of the club had grapevines and plenty of grapes on his own place, it was always a pleasure to steal those belonging to somebody else. On one occasion we visited Deacon Foster's vineyard. On the top of his fence, he had uprights with three strands of barbed-wire. To get over these was rather ticklish business, as one had to balance on one foot while the other foot was lifted over the barbed-wire and then balance again to get the other leg over. Many a pair of trousers came to grief on this fence! We took particular joy in raiding the Deacon's vineyard because he was no friend of us boys.

On one occasion, Billy Robinson and I were to get over the barbed-wire fence, collect the grapes, and toss them over to our two other confederates. Our friend the policeman interrupted the proceedings while Billy and I were in the grape-trellis. Of course, we had signals arranged, which were carried out by the use of the Punch and Judy whistle (two pieces of convex tin, covered with tape, with a piece of tape going through the center of the convexities). By putting this in the roof of the mouth when talking, the Punch and Judy voice was produced. While we were in the trellis, the Punch and Judy whistle was sounded by our "outposts," and Billy and I started to make our getaway, with our blouses filled with grapes. Billy, being quicker than I, reached the top of the fence and swung one leg over the wire, when the cop reached up, held him by the ankle, and told him to pull the other leg over and get down. Hearing this, I made off in the opposite direction, but in hurrying to get over the fence at another place, I fell and squashed most of the grapes which were in my blouse, and, at the same time, I swallowed my Punch and Judy whistle.

This was a very disturbing matter, as I presumed I would die with this whistle inside of me. At any rate, I got over the fence, only to be welcomed by another cop. Presently Billy's escort brought him over to where I was being held, and the two cops, with a firm hold on our collars, took us into the Deacon's living-room, where the old gentleman was having conversation with the Minister of the Negro Church. How much impression the Negro was making on the Deacon before our arrival I do not know, but he certainly took the opportunity to show his preaching powers, with Billy and me as his subject! He delivered an eloquent address on "Youth and Their Different Characters," of which ours were proven not the best. Deacon Foster applauded the Negro's sermon, and, I understood later gave him $500.00 for his church. The feature that amused us most afterwards was to learn that the Minister, after getting the $500.00, disappeared and was later arrested as a fakir. Of course, the officers took us to our respective homes, and we received further treatment from our fathers. I recollect clearly that Father asked me what was the matter with our grapes, and why we wanted to bother with Deacon Foster's. I really believe that he knew the answer, but under circumstances such as this I always found it wiser to make no replies to such enquiries.

One of these policemen became our arch enemy, and spoiled many of our tick-tack and shingle-games by surprising us when we were in the act of playing the tricks. Of course, we could not permit this. The streets were then dimly lighted by lanterns supported on wooden posts, in which were kerosene lamps. These lanterns did not throw much light. We used to attach a string to the post just beneath the lamp and carry it back onto a wall which was on Frank Slade's place. The string was arranged at just the right height to knock off the policeman's hat, which, in those days, was a high, conical helmet. This trick was played a great many times successfully, but eventually the eyes of the policeman became so sharpened that he would be on the lookout for the string. Sauntering along in an unconcerned manner, he would suddenly reach up, grab the string, and break it. He would then try to get up onto the wall in an attempt to catch us. In this he was never successful.

This trick having been played to the limit, we had to devise some other means of annoying him. We sawed through the base of the wooden lamp-post, leaving just enough to hold it in position. We tied a heavy clothes-line to the post at the same level that we usually placed the string and carried the clothesline back into the bushes above the wall, leaving the same set-up as with the string. The clothes-line, of course, was easily visible. When our friend the cop came along in the usual manner, making a bluff of not noticing the line, he would suddenly grab at it and pull the lamp-post down on top of himself, shattering the lantern and bursting the lamp within. Frequently the spilled oil caught on fire, which added to our joy. This was one of our very best tricks.

Of course, bean-blowers were included among our favorite amusements, and their use not confined to Hallowe'en. Many of the gentlemen in those days wore "plug hats," or "beavers," which offered attractive targets. Finding a satisfactory hiding-place near the sidewalk, we would pepper these toppers as certain unpopular gentlemen returned home in the evening. On one occasion the four of us let go all at once at one of these hats, which we thought was on the head of one of our most disliked neighbors. We made the error, however, in picking out the wrong man, as it turned out to be my father. While Father was usually broadminded in dealing with the deviltry of the boys, and was not usually an object of our pranks, he could not quite overlook this particular incident. I have reason to believe that he was more familiar with our doings than he ever admitted. In this particular case, being rather active on his feet, Father pounced down upon us, grabbing a couple of the bean-blowers, bending them up, and giving me and one other of the Gang very pronounced kicks in the pants. He had understanding enough to let us get away, feigning that he did not recognize us, thus avoiding the necessity of further action on his part.

FIREARMS and the instinct for hunting, of course, were a continuing urge. Some one of our Gang got hold of a gun known as the "Zulu" - just where, we never knew. At once it became the center of attraction. This was a single-barreled gun with a large breach-block and an enormous hammer. It carried the ordinary 12-gauge brass shell. My impression is that it was a modified Civil War, Springfield rifle. This weapon became the exciting cause of many expeditions whenever we could get ammunition for it, which was seldom. The privilege of shooting it was greatly coveted, and, when not in active use, we used to loan it among ourselves. It was a great event to have possession of it over night.

Muskrat hunting, back of Powder Horn Hill, on the marsh which now is beside the Revere Beach Boulevard, was one of our chief pastimes with this gun. Muskrats were plentiful, and, when we had a bad snowstorm in the early winter, shelldrake and whistlers (we did not know what they were then) used to come into these creeks.

On one occasion, when I had possession of the Zulu, I got up at perhaps three in the morning and walked to the marsh in back of the Marine Hospital (still located near Chelsea Bridge). My expedition was in search of ducks which I had noted were there in the evening and early morning. As this was my first hunting expedition alone, all my senses were keyed up, and nothing escaped my observation. Directly in back of the Marine Hospital was a large powder-magazine, which, as all we boys knew, was guarded. I was approaching it, in the dark, when there was a brilliant flash. This passed with great rapidity, but a bright glow lingered in the heavens for several seconds.

I immediately jumped to the idea that the powder magazine had blown up, and I knew that I would be in danger of being thought the cause of the catastrophe if I was found in that vicinity. Without further interest in the duck expedition, I rushed home as fast as my legs would carry me and took refuge in my bed. I was completely perplexed that no reference was made to it next morning. I took the opportunity that day to visit the magazine district and found the building still intact. The next morning Father read in the paper at breakfast that a large meteor had fallen somewhere in the West. Meteors were unknown to me, but an interest in them was immediately created. I became quite a person in the minds of the rest of the Gang for having actually seen one fall.

This Zulu-gun got us into considerable trouble, probably the most distressing event being when Walter Walker and I killed a lot of pigeons. Near a large public school on Broadway, in Chelsea, there was a wooden dwelling-house on which the pigeons used to congregate in great numbers, usually in the afternoon. This house, being located on the principal street in the city, and on which horse-cars ran, was hardly a secluded spot. Walter and I had planned the killing of these pigeons for a long time, and finally we obtained some powder and shot. We loaded several brass shells, which we used in this gun, appropriated Mother's wicker clothes-basket, and proceeded down Broadway to the house where they gathered.

Arriving, we found the roof well covered with pigeons. From the sidewalk we took a shot at them. Several birds, as well as some pieces of the shingles, came rolling off the roof. We collected the dead birds and chased several of the wounded ones. Our spoils were deposited in the clothes-basket, and we waited a short time until the pigeons again congregated on the roof. Not only did the pigeons gather, but as school had just let out, we were quickly surrounded by a crowd of children, as well as a few grown-ups who seemed to be interested but who did not interfere with our sport.

We got two or three more shots, and had the basket well filled with pigeons, when we saw a cop coming down the street. This was a signal for us to cease operations, and, without telling the crowd that the show was over, we grabbed our basket and disappeared through back-yards and down alleys until we finally reached Walter's house as we thought in safety. It was not long, however, before the policeman and some kids put in an appearance. We assured the cop that we were entirely innocent. There was no trace of the gun or basket of birds. However, some of the kids had seen our performance, and told the cop not to believe us. We found out afterwards that one of these children lived in the house where we had been shooting the pigeons. The policeman explained to Mrs. Walker what had been done, and Mr. Walker and my father were sent for. When they arrived at Walter's home, they were informed by Mrs. Walker that they would find us in the lockup. The policeman did not put us in the cells, but we were detained in the police station until our parents appeared. This ended the Zulu. While the gun did not belong to Walter or me, it was never seen again. Just what became of the pigeons also still remains a mystery.

FOR one of my early misdemeanors, I have always believed that I was cruelly misunderstood. Whether or not boys have a sense of patriotism in an unusual degree I am not sure. I am rather inclined to believe that this is true. Like all intangible emotional things, reason does not, as a rule, play an important part. A soldier had always been the object of my boyish admiration and respect. One day, when I was watching a G. A. R. parade, one of the soldiers fell on the sidewalk near me. I picked him up and took him into the Hotel Vendome to get him off the street. I did not realize at the time that he was drunk, but thought he had fainted. I felt very proud to have the privilege come to me of taking care of this soldier man, being filled with the idea that he must be a great hero, who had fought for his country, and all that. Later in the day, when he had partially recovered, I took him home and put him to bed in our guest-room.

The family happened to be out, and when they returned and found that I had installed a strange man in the house, even the fact that he was a soldier in the Grand Army made no hit. My patriotism received a rude shock. I refused to believe the family when they insisted that I did not know what kind of man I had brought home, and that he might be a very bad character for all I knew. To complete my disillusion, this turned out to be the case. When the man sobered up, he went wandering around the house, becoming boisterous and insulting, and after we gave him breakfast we had to get a policeman to eject him. I have since learned that soldiers may be of varying character, and the fact that a man is or has been a soldier does not necessarily place him on a pedestal.

AMONG my family's greatest friends were the Harwoods, who lived in Lynn. It was the habit for Mother and Father to dine with them every Wednesday night, the Harwoods dining with us every Sunday night. Father and Mother used to drive down across the Lynn Turnpike regularly each Wednesday afternoon in a Goddard buggy. The Harwoods had a son, Charles, and he and I were thrown much together. While somewhat older than I, he had not lost his interest in gunpowder and weapons, and I believe my very earliest experience with a rifle was with him. He had a Flobert rifle, an inexpensive, 22-caliber gun, which was in common use with the boys of that day. I often went to Lynn and spent Friday night with Charlie, and on Saturday morning we would walk on the beach leading to Little Nahant. There we would crawl down on the rocks and pop at the ducks, but, so far as I can recollect, we never hit one.

On one occasion we were going out to Little Nahant over the railroad-track, the large part of which was on a trestle, as it went over the marsh and creeks. How I happened to be alone I do not recollect, but while I was on one of these trestles, I saw a train approaching. As there was but a single track, with little room on the sides, my only means of escape from being run over was to slip down between the beams and hang suspended over the water while the train passed over me. Just how I was able to do this is now a mystery, and how I was able to crawl back is beyond my comprehension. Charlie had watched the procedure with great apprehension, and, of course, thought I had dropped off into the river. This was an event we decided not to discuss with the family on our return.

Charles Harwood had two friends, Bert Gamble and Dick Lord, who were likewise interested in gunpowder. One day we four filled a quart tin milk-can with blasting powder, wadded it in heavily with cloth and paper, and fixed a fuse into it through a heavy, wooden milk-stopper. We buried this bomb, with the fuse sticking up above the surface, in Mother Harwood's garden, which was but a few yards from the house. The fuse was lighted several times, but it kept going out. Bert was approaching the now stubby fuse to light it again, when off went the bomb. The wooden stopper struck him in the shoulder and broke his arm. He was also very badly scarred and was confined to the hospital for some time. Most of the windows in the back of the house were shattered, and that ended my visits to Charlie for a long time, yet the four of us had many escapades together. Dick Lord being the most adventurous, was always my chosen companion. Through a curious coincidence, while I was surgeon at the Boston City Hospital many years later, I was called to the East

Boston Relief Station to take care of a case of fractured skull and found the victim to be my old friend Dick Lord. He, still looking for adventure, even with advancing years, had crashed his automobile into a telegraph pole while driving at great speed.

THE first summer activities that I can remember were at Mount Vernon, New Hampshire, when I was about six or seven years old. The only outstanding event in connection with this inland summer-resort was in connection with a Fourth of July celebration, the first one I remember. In the evening they were having fireworks, shooting off Roman candles, and lighting colored lights. Somebody, probably Father, gave me what he supposed was a Roman candle. This was lighted, and I was holding it in my hand, shaking it with the idea of seeing the balls come out. Unfortunately, it turned out to be a light, and, as I shook it, some of the molten material went into my left eye. The feature that I remember particularly about it must have been some days later, when the Doctor removed the bandage. Father was holding me, and, putting his hand over my right eye, shook me, and, in a very excited voice, asked me if I could see out of the damaged eye. When I proved to him that I could, I remember his putting me down, and, trying to hide the fact that he was crying, he left the room. The eye has been all right since, but the scar still remains.

EVERY new servant who came to the house had to be initiated. As there were no electric lights in those days, the houses were lighted by gas, and the matches, which were kept in metal boxes with covers, came in packages of cards, the match itself having a phosphorous tip, and below it a layer of sulphur about three-quarters of an inch deep. They were commonly called "hell-sticks," and made much smell when they were lighted. The phosphorus and sulphur, when rubbed on a moist surface, would produce a glow in the dark.

The initiation of new servants consisted of taking some of these hell-sticks and rubbing them about our eyes and along our noses and around our lips. After the girl went to bed, we used to sneak into her room with our faces thus decorated and wake her up. As most of these girls were Catholics, their reaction to what they saw was usually loud prayers and calls on the Saints, and especially on those saints who seemed to have the greatest influence with the Devil. More than one maid refused to stay in our house after this initiation.

A variation of the initiation was to take a small cannon, which we loaded with blasting powder, and place it at the top of the stairs where we knew the maid would go by. From this we ran a string from the trigger across the hall, so that when she came along, she would hit it and explode the gun. This trick we usually played when the family was away. On the one occasion which the family witnessed, the explosion startled everyone in the house as well as the servant. The gun was promptly confiscated and the reprimand severe. But we were versatile. After losing the cannon, this same trick was played by balancing a can of marbles on the top step, so that when the maid upset it with the string the marbles would go bouncing down, making sufficient noise to gratify our desire to be disturbing.

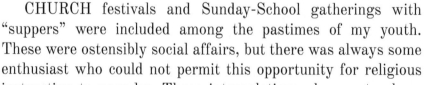

CHURCH festivals and Sunday-School gatherings with "suppers" were included among the pastimes of my youth. These were ostensibly social affairs, but there was always some enthusiast who could not permit this opportunity for religious instruction to pass by. These interpolations always struck us boys as taking an unfair advantage of us, and we promptly retaliated.

On one occasion I remember, in company with a large group of other children, I had to listen to a long talk on some religious subject by Miss T., who was in charge of the Sunday-School activities. After making an address which was infinitely more impressive to her than to the rest of us, she asked all present who believed in what she had said to stand up. Just why I became rebellious at that moment I do not know, but I do remember that I did not like what she said or her manner of expressing it. Everybody else stood except myself. To make matters worse as far as I was concerned, Miss T. drew attention to me, and insisted on knowing why I did not rise. I had no ready answer, and she made what I thought unnecessary personal remarks directed entirely at me. This increased my contrariness. As I would make no response to any of her enquiries, she finally very pointedly asked me if I was a Christian. I felt strongly that her attitude was not Christian-like, and, being driven to make some answer, I told her that I considered myself a Christian, but certainly not on her standard.

This caused quite a disturbance, and as punishment Miss T. decreed that, when the good things to eat were served in the vestry, I would have to wait on everybody else and have none myself. So, when we all went to the vestry, I had to pass the ice-cream and cake. Miss T. was an Amazonian type of woman. On this occasion she wore very tight corsets and a very low neck. Somehow a plate of ice-cream, quite soft, which I was passing, happened to slip and ran down her exposed neck and breasts as she sat talking to one of the children. Of course, this was a pure accident, but I was too good a Christian to be sorry, so I did not apologize.

I recall another incident associated with my Church memories. Mrs. Albert Bossom, a most kindly soul, interested in music and the activities of the First Baptist Church on Carey Avenue, Chelsea, had, for many years, conducted the choir in this church. I became one of the boy sopranos in her choir. The rehearsals were held at Mrs. Bossom's house in the evening. She always furnished refreshments, and the group of boys became very friendly. Harold Tripp, who has become one of the best tenors in this country, was a member of this group, and my particular girl playmate, Geraldine Farrar, occasionally joined with us. She afterwards became one of the most famous of our American Opera singers. Geraldine and I were very chummy, and one of our greatest pastimes was to make candy in our kitchen.

This boys' choir must have been pretty good, as we took part in many concerts in Boston and elsewhere. One of these occasions was at a large gathering of Baptists at Tremont Temple. We sang early in the program and were dismissed from the stage while the speaking continued. Being at large, and restless and inquisitive as usual, Harold Tripp and I started on a tour of investigation of the building. On our rambles we landed in the basement, where we found a room filled with large switches. This evidently was a control room for the lighting of the hall and the whole building. These switches interested us, and we began playing with them. While we were still carrying on our experiments, we heard someone hurrying down the basement steps. Disappearing into a coalbin, we watched him rush into the control-room. After we rejoined the other members of the choir, we learned that, while somebody was giving a very heated religious speech, all the lights went out. We were told that it came at a most appropriate time in the speech, as the orator was talking about darkness and light. We were undiscovered, but much frightened.

Another similar escapade occurred when Mrs. Bossom, who was a friend of the wife of the then Governor of the State, took us to the Governor's house for a concert. The Governor's wife was convalescing from a long illness, and Mrs. Bossom's thought was that it would be pleasant for her to hear the boys sing. During the evening, when we were at leisure, Billy Robinson, Harold Tripp, and I thought we would make an investigation of the house. We had ventured into several dark rooms, and were greatly interested in our burglarious activities, although we took nothing. We opened many doors, some of which went into vacant rooms, others into closets, and really were having a grand time when we ventured into a very dimly lighted room. As we went by a bed in this room, a woman began yelling, "Murder." Needless to say, we started to get away as rapidly as possible. Apparently, we had gotten into the room of the Governor's wife and had frightened her almost to death. Harold was caught by a butler, but Billy and I escaped.

Our organist at the church, who was a great friend of ours, was taken ill, and a substitute, whom we did not like, took his place. He was very disagreeable to us. It seemed to annoy him to have us sitting in the choir-seats near the organ, so he made us retire to a small room behind the organ. We all resented this, as we enjoyed looking out into the church and seeing what was going on. We put up with it as long as we thought reasonable and then decided something ought to be done about it.

On one Sunday he left the door to the back of the organ unlocked. Harold Tripp and I, being the ones who usually pulled off the tricks, got in back of the organ, and, while the organist was making the instrument roar, we began to pull the various stops in quick succession. As both of us were at it with both hands, we changed his program considerably. The organ simply went wild. The organist tried his best to get the stops back, but as he would pull them one way we would pull them the other. It gave the audience quite an experience. The organist had to keep going -with his piece, but when he had brought it to an end he rushed back, with strong suspicion as to what had been going on. He found us all sitting innocently in our seats.

OTHER PURSUITS

As mentioned earlier, my father was an avid sportsman. He hunted in the Fall and fished all Summer. I was lucky enough to start tagging along with him at a very early age. One of the earliest, when I was five or six, was riding with my father who was taking my grandfather, Dr. John H Cunningham, to The Tihonet Club. Tihonet was/is a trout fishing club that leased land from the Makepeace Company, which owned thousands of acres of cranberry bogs. The retention ponds that were used to keep the bogs irrigated and flooded for picking were stocked with trout. This was in Wareham, MA, and a short drive from my grandparents' house, Sandham, at Long Beach. It was also another world when compared to being at the edge of Buzzards Bay. Rather than the smell of the marshes and the bay, once you crossed Route 28, the air seem drier, and the scent of the scrub pine forest was dominant. It was a wild and intriguing place to me.

The Tihonet Club is one of the oldest trout fishing clubs in the country and had a long list of very prominent members. In those days, much of the fishing took place in the main water channels down the cranberry bogs. I was like most five or six year-olds, very active and wanting to see everything going on. No one had told me not to go behind anyone fly casting, not that I would have listened anyway. Yes, on my very first fishing expedition, my grandfather hooked me on the back cast, much to his disgruntlement as he was casting to a rising fish. He had been a surgeon and he deftly removed the hook from my arm. While there was some pain, the worst part was feeling like everyone was mad at me. A few years later, I had the chance to make up for this and row my grandfather around the Frogfoot reservoir as he trolled for the elusive monster brown trout. Both my father and I joined the Tihonet Club later in life. It was a source of much pleasure and many hours spent fishing for trout and hunting for grouse. As cancer was taking its final toll on him, I got my father out for his last trip to Tihonet. Unable to stand, he was seated in a lawn chair on the flume structure at the base of the Frogfoot Reservoir so he could cast out into the pond. Therefore, my first freshwater fishing trip with my father was at the Tihonet Club as was our last. The Club was also where my son, C. M. "Gil" Cunningham III, caught his first flyrod trout in the exact place that I had been hooked by my grandfather.

The author's son, Gil Cunningham, with his first Tihonet trout at the exact spot where the author caught his own first trout using the very same tackle and was hooked forevermore by his grandfather.

As the years went on, I hunted and fished a lot with my father, learning all the necessary skills and techniques. On Old Farm Rd, only two other boys in our group had the same kind of experience, Spider Andresen and Phil Reed.

The Andresens had moved from Dedham to Duxbury, MA. In some ways it seemed like they had truly moved a long distance away, but we still got together almost every weekend during the duck hunting season to spend a night out on the marsh and the hunting stand called the Roney Plaza. It was named after the Miami Beach hotel near the Fontainebleau. As the season changed from summer fishing to fall hunting, we would spend a weekend or two getting the hunting house on stilts and the contiguous walkways completely grassed up with elephant grass (phragmites) and corn stalks. This took many loads in the Andresen's high sided and flat-bottomed skiff. It was usually done with a decent sized group of others who hoped to be asked to come and hunt.

Once the season started, I vividly remember the Friday evening ritual of driving to Duxbury. Then getting the boat launched into the back marsh area in the dark and loading all the gear for hunting as well as our food and duffle was a chore done in freezing cold weather and sometimes with rain or snow. It didn't matter, we'd be hunting the following day. I do not remember how many years we hunted there, but a lot. Then one summer around the Fourth of July, someone torched the building on stilts. I am told it was a heck of a blaze, but also the end of the Roney Plaza. Spider's dad, John was devastated by the loss. It had meant a lot to him and after that happened he stopped hunting altogether. The stilt building was replaced by a house barge that was floated into place and secured there. It was never really the same. It served a similar function for lodging on site, but it did not have the same feeling. I am not positive, but I think that the barge was lost in a storm and that ended our use of the property in the way we had for years. Spider and I inherited the two marsh islands and only occasionally went there to hunt. Years later we sold the property to North's brother, Linc Lyman, and his friend, Cap Kane. There is no hunting infrastructure there today. The marsh has reclaimed what minimal impact we had.

During our hunting on the Duxbury marsh, there was one other gunning stand as they were called. It belonged to Bill Ellison, another Duxbury resident with very deep pockets. There was always some friendly competition between the hunting stands. We were a little closer to the bay, so we had the first attempt to get the ducks to decoy. But "Wild Bill" as he was known had all the toys. He had electric callers and didn't mind using them to lure ducks away from us. On rare occasions we'd go over for a visit, and he had a much fancier house and a TV to watch football games. Behind the house was a domed building that had a roof opening and held a big telescope. He was a very competitive person and was involved in a wide variety of sports. I shot competitive skeet with and against him in later years.

Just by chance, when the Andresens moved out of Dedham, the Reeds moved from High St. to Old Farm Rd. So, my other fishing and occasionally hunting friend, Phil Reed, and I took our learned skills and put them to use. All the money that we made selling soda pop or mail order seeds or homemade pies went to fishing tackle. Some of it came from Keenan's hardware store in downtown Dedham Square. They did not have a great selection, but they had enough to help us fill our tackle boxes. What Keenan's did not have, we were able to send away for and get mail order. In those days, you did not just get on your laptop or mobile phone and order. You had to look through a magazine or two or three and find a place that sold fishing supplies. Then write a letter ordering a catalog. Then if they had exactly what you wanted, you filled out an order blank and mailed it back with a money order for the items. It took a while and caused a great deal of excitement when the products finally arrived.

Phil and I walked to a couple of easily accessible ponds or other bodies of water and did some fishing there. One of the most accessible areas was the Charles River and it provided us with a number of possibilities. We spent a lot of time at the Dedham Water Company pumping station which was next to the Bridge Street river crossing. We caught a few bass, the odd pickerel and a ton of sunfish. There was a little channel that came off the river and ran up toward the pumping station. One side was mowed grass and the other was swampy brush that was mostly flooded. We noticed that there were occasional black water snakes cruising along the brush in the channel. So, we decided to catch a few. We'd take a small sunfish and tie a piece of monofilament to its lower jaw, flip the sunfish out in the channel and tie off the end. Then we'd leave this overnight. We'd return the next day to see what we had. A few times things were broken off, but often we'd have caught a decent sized water snake. Snakes are not able to regurgitate, so we'd simply pull them in. Hold them behind the head and pull the remainder of the sunfish out and let the snake go. Phil told his father, Loring, about our snake catching. His father had some connection to the Museum of Science in Boston. It just so happened that they wanted some black water snakes for a display. No problem. I think we sold four or five and got a few bucks for each. That income went right back into more tackle. Then one day we were down at our usual place and fishing had been slow. Phil decided to lie down facing the edge of the channel and try to grab a snake swimming by. After a while a snake was cruising down the middle of the channel, minding its own business, and Phil reached out to grab it. Well, he did not get it near the head, but just about the middle. It turned out not to be a water snake, but a big ribbon snake. When Phil grabbed him, he whipped around and bit Phil on the mouth just above and below his lips. He quickly tossed the snake back in the water and headed home, teary eyed and lightly bleeding. We decided to leave the snakes alone and focus our efforts on fish. But later in life, Phil would not be deterred. He went to school in Arizona and returned to his Dedham house with a rattlesnake. I keenly remember going down to his room in the cellar and he calmly said to me that his rattlesnake was loose somewhere in the room, but he wasn't sure where. My visit was short, but I stayed up on the bed out of striking distance. Snakes in general did not bother me, but ones that were poisonous certainly got my attention. And ones that were poisonous and not visible required great care. Phil eventually found the snake and returned it to its cage. I believe that his mother laid down the law and said no more poisonous snakes. Phil was returning the rattler to Arizona and had it in a carry-on bag. Carry-ons were not inspected in those days. As he waited to board the plane, he suddenly noticed that someone had taken the carry-on. They were about to be surprised. Many years later, while hunting quail in South Carolina with my father-in-law, Ted Lyman, and my son, Gil, I had an unplanned run in with a rattler. I was walking along and watching the hunting dogs that had just busted a covey of quail, when something told me to look down in mid stride. There right in my path and just out of its underground hole was a massive rattlesnake. Its head was as large as my hand laid flat on a surface. The largest part of its body was bigger around than my two hands forming a circle. If I had stepped on it, I would have been bitten and in serious trouble. I stepped back and shot most of its head off. Holding its tail as high as possible, the remainder of its head was still on the ground. For months I woke up in the night in a cold sweat just thinking about what almost happened. I digress.

 So, now during the summers, we were fully focused on fishing. Phil's parents had a bicycle built for two that they never used. For us this was a very fancy bike. It had 3 gears, while our old bikes had only one. Phil talked them into adding wire baskets on either side of the rear wheel. This was going to be our transportation to every body of water we could find in rideable range. We added rod holders to the baskets. Then we'd put tackle boxes and lunch in the baskets, load the rods and we were good to go.

 The first destinations were ones that we knew about. Back to the Charles River where we could get access to Motley's Pond. We caught some nice pickerel and a few largemouth bass. Somehow, we figured out that there was a pond on the Stone estate off of Louder Street. It was always called Stone's Pond to us, but I believe the given name was Rodman Pond. We rode up the long drive and could see the pond which had been posted. It looked awesome. So we decided to ride up the house, knock on the door, introduce ourselves and ask permission. Mrs. Stone who was approximately our grandmothers' age had us come into the house. I should say mansion. It was beautiful and her living room windows overlooked the pond. We explained who we were, where we lived, and that we'd like to be able to fish in the pond. We promised not to keep any fish and not to leave any litter and that it would only be the two of us. Much to our surprise and delight, we were given permission with the caveat of not too early and not too late. No problem. Shortly after, we got the first taste of what would be our go to destination. OMG. The pond had some very nice sized bass and also pickerel. For us, a three or four pound bass was amazing and they were readily available. We learned a lot about technique there. What lures worked and what changes made them better. We learned what to look for in terms of where the fish hung out and where they fed. Also, where to catch bass and where to catch pickerel. It was the most exciting place we would ever find, and it was our first ask and ultimately our personal place to fish. Several times other guys who would try to sneak in by the dam at the foot of the pond and we would quietly let the property caretaker know. The trespassers would soon be gone.

    We continued to explore. We knew about Harding's Pond off Westfield Street, which in those days went all the way past the Dedham Country & Polo Club, since there was yet to be a Route 128, now Route 95. The pond was named Weld Pond, but since we knew the Hardings who lived on the pond, that was our name. For us the access was around the Harding property and while the fishing there was ok, we were missing a lot. We tried the normal asking permission process but got shot down by a couple of folks and decided to move on.

    Heading further out on Westfield St, we made it to the Dedham Country & Polo Club skating rink ponds. Today, these ponds are filled in and overgrown, but in those days they were wide open with water access to the Charles River. They had an unending supply of largemouth bass. None of these were too large as there were likely too many in there, but the challenge was to walk a plank from the shore out to the permanent hockey boards and balance there while casting and catching. When we wanted lunch, we could sit on the porch of the warming hut and eat whatever we had brought. For some reason, we never thought about going to the Club and ordering a sandwich at the pool snack shop.

One summer around this time, my uncle, Stewart Woodworth, had organized a summer camping trip to the Canadian Maritimes. I was asked if I wanted to join them with their son, Woody. I had never done anything like that and quickly joined in.

We drove through New Brunswick and then around Nova Scotia. Early in the trip, Uncle Stewart had arranged guided fishing for Atlantic salmon on the St Mary's River. I do not remember the town we were in, but we camped right on the river. My uncle had booked two days of fly fishing. On the first day, Woody and I were exploring along the river bank. A much bigger teenage boy came out of the woods with a spinning rod and a can of worms. He glowered at us, so we kept our distance, but I was very curious about watching him fish. It didn't take too long before his rod bent, and we saw a sizeable fish jumping in the river. He put maximum pressure on the fish and soon beached it. He grabbed the fish and turned to us, and threatened bodily harm if we said a word to anyone. He disappeared back into the woods with his fish. Wow, I thought that was pretty cool.

Having dinner that night, we told Uncle Stewart what we had seen because he was complaining about not seeing a fish all day. He grumbled that what the boy had done was illegal as it was fly fishing only. The next day was sunny and warm. At lunchtime, Uncle Stewart came in for a while and said that we could go out and try our luck for an hour. I had brought my first fly rod and reel with me. It was a 6 weight Shakespeare rod and a Hardy reel set up for trout. Not what you want for catching a strong fish, but that didn't matter as we were just being allowed out to fill some time. The guide anchored the boat, pointed out where the salmon were and promptly went to sleep on the bow. Woody did not fish, so it was all me. The guide had tied on a big white Wulff dry fly. I was a decent caster, but it took a little bit to get used to the big fly. As I cast and cast and cast again for what seemed like an eternity, I was looking down in the water and could see the weed bed waving in the the current. Where were the fish? I wondered. Then suddenly, as plain as day, a dark fish shape rose from the weeds. As it got closer to the surface, it lightened into a silver monster. I watched in awe as its head broke the surface and inhaled my fly. I set the hook and hollered something. The guide woke up but couldn't get the anchor up with enough speed. The salmon smoked off all my fly line in several crashing jumps. The line came tight on the reel arbor, and the leader broke. The guide shook his head and mumbled something about being a 25-pound fish. We went back ashore with an amazing story and the newly planted Atlantic salmon seed. My uncle never saw a fish.

Atlantic salmon on a dry fly by the author.

Up on Strawberry Hill in Dover, my maternal grandparents had a farm which also had a pond in which were largemouth bass. I do not exactly remember if we stocked that pond with fish from another pond, but I do know that we took fish from that pond years later and stocked other new or barren ponds in the area. One at my parents' house next door and another pond my grandfather had dug upstream from the older one.

Several of us had also gotten into building battery powered boats out of sheet balsa and other balsa pieces. They were usually about 2 feet long and shaped like a PT boat. Some of them had electric inboard engines and some had electric outboards. We'd cruise them across my grandparents' pond to a waiting person and they'd get turned around and sent back. Since they were not all that fast, we got the idea of putting on a 3 ft length of monofilament and attaching some sort of spinner to the end. Then off the boat would go trolling the spinner. Quite often, a fish would be hooked and then the tug of war was on. If the boat did not run out of battery, it won. On several occasions, we had to get a rod and cast a lure over the boat and retrieve the whole mess and release the fish. We were always concerned that a very big fish would sink the boat.

One time when I was with Sandy Darrell, from the Dedham neighborhood, the boat was stopped in its tracks, luckily near the bank, and almost pulled under. Holy smokes, we thought that we'd hooked a monster. Well, we had, but it wasn't a fish. It was a snapping turtle that had grabbed our hooked fish for a snack. We could see the snapper down on the bottom not too far from shore. I ran up to the garage and grabbed a net that for whatever reason hung there. I drew the short straw and had to wade into the pond and scoop the turtle up in the net. Of course, the act of wading stirred up a lot of bottom sediment. The first attempt got the turtle in, but he was not too happy and managed to escape into the muddy water around me. Now I was concerned that I could become his next snack. Suddenly, I saw movement right down in front of me. I made a wild swipe with the net and could feel the snapper thrashing inside. Sandy and I dragged it up on the bank and then to the garage and wondered what would be next. My grandparents were not at home, but I knew that my grandfather had seen the turtle and commented that he hoped the turtle did not eat the wood duck ducklings that hatched out each Spring. I knew that my grandfather had a very beautiful .25 caliber automatic pistol with pearl handles and being inquisitive, I knew where he stored it. So, I got it out of his gun closet, loaded it and we dispatched the turtle. Although the turtle was dead, its muscles continued to move for a day or so. We found that a little spooky, but also interesting. Later on, I informed my grandfather who was pleased that the turtle was no longer a threat to the ducklings in the pond. I did not mention the pistol, but he seemed happy enough that if I had mentioned it, I would have been ok.

Sandy Darrell and the Author at the farm with the offending snapping turtle. Author is also holding the .25 cal pistol.

As with many things we did growing up, the pond fishing in all its variations began to change to salt water fishing with our parents. That was a new and exciting experience, and the fish were a lot bigger. Little did I know what that would mean for later in life.

MORE COUNTRY ADVENTURE

We discovered that there were a lot of things to do around the farm. While we liked the fishing, we had not forgotten our interest in guns. On the farm, as noted earlier there was the old dump where the family who owned the property before my grandparents deposited some trash, mostly metal containers and bottles of all shapes and sizes. These were perfect targets for our BB guns and if we got lucky a .22 caliber rifle. Over some time, we probably destroyed what today would be hundreds of dollars' worth of antique bottles. I remember many of them being beautiful dark blue glass, much like the famous Sandwich glass that is coveted today. We used this target range until my parents built their new house, which was almost on top of the old dump.

We also spent some time poking around in the attic of my grandparents' house. There were all sorts of military uniforms from both WWI and WWII. My grandfather had been an Army officer during WWI. His dress sword was a thing of beauty. We also found a couple of old muzzle loading rifles. They could have been handed down from someone who participated in the Civil War. They had bayonets that could be fixed in the outward or inward position. So, we got to thinking about these guns and trying to figure out how they worked. We asked my grandfather if we could try to fire one of the rifles. He seemed amused that we thought we could figure it out and then actually fire one of them. So, he agreed.

What he did not know was that we had access to powder from firecrackers and also could scavenge some 12 gauge shotgun shells. Firecracker powder would be used as propellant. The shotgun shells would be cut in half and the lead shot melted and poured back into the end of the casing. The solidified lead cut out of the casing would make the projectile that would just slide down the barrel. Then we'd pack in the powder with a small piece of cloth as wadding. Then add the projectile. The biggest question was how much powder and since we did not have any caps to ignite the powder, we would use a firecracker fuse inserted into the nipple that would normally hold the ignition cap. We were also concerned about the gun blowing up with too much powder, so we simply tied it to a tree and lit the fuse. The first attempt luckily sent the projectile out the barrel, but it only went about a hundred feet or so. If there had not been enough powder and the projectile stuck in the barrel, that would have been game over. So, after the first firing we doubled the powder load and tried again. The bang was a lot more impressive, and we could hear the slug going through the trees at the end of the field. Ok, that was cool, and we had proven our point of successfully firing it.

There were other things around the farm that would keep a boy's attention. First and foremost was the maintenance shop in the garage next to the barn. Bill Morris, who was the farm foreman, was quite grumpy about us getting into the shop and messing with tools, etc. So, we'd figure out a time when he would be working out in the vegetable garden or on the tractor mowing. Then we'd look around to see what we might be able to build. After the success with the muzzleloader, we decided to see if we could build something to use with cherry bombs or ashcans. We found a 3 ft piece of metal pipe That had threading on one end. It was the perfect size to accept a golf ball. We also found a cap that matched the size and threading to close off one end. Then, we were all set to test this bad boy out. What we had crafted was a crude mortar. We leaned it up against a stone wall and braced it with some rocks. In went the lit cherry bomb and down went the golf ball. Boom and the golf ball was out of site. The concussion jerked the pipe around quite a bit. We braced it with more rocks, which held. Then we tried to have it fire a little closer to level. That time we could hear the golf ball bouncing off the trees. A lot later in life, I found some of the golf balls and they were an impressive distance into the woods. Then, we reckoned that if we could make a cannon that was able to be aimed, we'd really have something. Back to the shop we went and cobbled together a way to aim the barrel up or down and a little left or right. On the first shot, the golf ball was visible and the longest hitter in golf would have been impressed. The whole device did jerk back some. I had the second shot. Light it, drop it in and add the golf ball in a matter of seconds. I took aim at the end of the field. I never did see the golf ball as our shoddy craftsmanship came completely apart and the barrel flew back over my right shoulder. If it had hit me, there would have been severe damage. Ducked another bullet, so to speak, and concluded that we had gone as far as we could with this little project. We returned all the pieces to the farm shop.

Sometime shortly after the mortar escapade, we began to get interested in things on wheels. I think that someone in the Old Farm Rd neighborhood built a Soap Box Derby car and that was the spark that lit our fire. Phil Reed was definitely a major mover in this effort. We crafted what was supposed to be a derby qualifying car. I doubt that it was, since we were not following any of the strict instructions. Again, we used some of the tools in the farm garage. When we got it finished or as finished as we could so that it would roll forward with someone steering. Then we'd run it down Strawberry Hill Street from the barn, past the junction of Wilsondale and on down a way. My cousin, Bob Truesdale, was also involved in this project since his family then lived at 35 Strawberry Hill St on part of the farm. The coasting down the hill was fun for a while, but the necessity to bring it back up every time got old. We wanted something with an engine.

It just so happened that there was an old walk behind gas powered reel style mower that had some major mechanical issue in the cutting apparatus, but the engine worked fine. So, again much to Bill Morris's dismay, we appropriated the motor. While Bill was less than amused with our poking around the farm shop, he had come to need our help during the summer. There were two large hayfields on the farm, and they were cut and baled twice a summer. Bill got Jerry Cronin who lived and worked on a farm next door to run the tractor that towed the baling machine. Bill ran the flatbed truck following behind and several of us young boys would sling the bales up on the truck. From the truck they would have to transferred to the hay loft. This happened in June then again later in the summer. We got Cokes and sometimes cookies for our efforts. Bill and Jerry would quietly down some cold beer. On one occasion, Bill decided to start the seasonal processing of the chickens. We soon learned the true meaning of running around like a chicken with its head cut off. He thought it was amusing. We thought it completely gross.

Back to our mechanical endeavors, we somehow managed to build a belt drive clutch system that worked by depressing a peddle to tighten the belt. The other foot ran the accelerator which changed the engine speed a little, but those old Briggs & Stratton motors were not designed for high rpms. Since our biggest concern was to get this contraption to move forward, we had no brake. We never really needed one since our full throttle forward speed was less than that of a strong marathon runner. The other problem was that our crude clutching system ate up belts with great regularity and of course we wanted more speed. Over a short period, our less than perfect workmanship was evidenced in major structural failures in the wood framed "go kart." This project was scrapped, and the engine was returned to the farm garage to be used as a spare or for parts. But that was not the end to our four wheeled endeavors. We quickly realized that we needed to have a metal frame go kart with all the necessary parts, but how to accomplish that was the question. I don't recall the exact timing, but if memory serves, Uncle Pie Truesdale, Bob's father, bought the first real go kart. Pie was a kid at heart and got a real kick out of the same kinds of things that we did. I believe that the go kart was meant for Bill Truesdale, Bob's younger brother. There were a lot of miles put on that go kart around the farm driveways. Someone even tried to make a track out in one of the hayfields, but the low clearance of the kart was a real problem. However, the flame was lit. As we got a little older, we put together faster and faster karts. The last of which had two engines, centrifugal clutches with chain drives and ran on alcohol and castor oil. We eventually raced some of these at a track in Bourne, MA just over the Bourne Bridge onto Cape Cod. I eventually went on to other interests, but Phil Reed kept at it with an unfulfilled appetite for speed. He went on to race some twin engine karts that would reach 80 mph. Even as this is written, he has an electric kart that is faster than any gas powered he had and also an all-electric Tesla Plaid EV with 1000 hp, which can reach 60 mph in under 3 seconds. Plus a C8 Corvette that he took to racing school. He still races motor cross and crushes the competition with his Tesla.

As for me, this early vehicle interest fueled my own somewhat muted, in comparison to Phil's, addiction to cars. Up through my college years, I owned a number of different cars. I wish I had kept all of them. I had one of the original 1964 Ford Mustang hard tops. A Lotus Elite from the mid '50s that had won its class at Le Mans. It was an amazing car to drive with a very high rpm Coventry Climax engine. It was right hand drive, and the top of the roof only came to my waist. Another different car was a dark Maroon 1952 Cadillac combination hearse and ambulance. There were metal signs that mounted inside the rear windows declaring what the vehicle was. I bought that off a fellow student who had to get rid of it as he was put on academic probation. I might have paid $100, but it was in beautiful condition and ran well. On some Saturday evenings, we would put a bunch of fraternity friends and dates in the back and go to the drive-in movie theater with curtains drawn and the Ambulance signs in the windows. By getting static on the radio between stations, I'd pretend that I was on ambulance duty and get in for free. Then we would back into our space and open up the back door and watch the movie. One time, my parents, Mac and Babsie, came to visit at Rollins College. We were going out to dinner at a restaurant, so my date and I picked up my parents at the hotel with the 52 Caddy. My father was amused, but when I opened the side door to allow them to get into the vehicle, my mother almost flatly refused to. She thought the idea of sitting in the "jump seats" next to the casket table was appalling. My father convinced her after a while and off we went to dinner. My guess is that she was concerned that someone would see her getting out of the hearse/ambulance.

During those college years, I would also own several motorcycles. One was a British Small Arms (BSA) 650 cc 1960 model and the other was a Triumph Bonneville 650 cc. Both very nice rides.

I would eventually leave college with no car and no motorcycles and have regretted it ever since. How I would like to have all of them today! Hindsight is almost perfect, although I would have had to build a barn to contain them all. Ah, well. Onward.

FINALLY GROWING UP—A LITTLE

The ticking clock makes growing older impossible to resist, but growing up is more a state of mind. Even as I slid my way through primary and secondary school, I did not so much resist growing up, I ignored it.

There is not a lot I remember about grade school at Dedham Country Day school. Certainly, some of my classmates were friends for a few years, but only two of the Old Farm Road gang went to DCD. One incident that I do vividly recall was a girl in my class, Penny Crittenden, whose family lived next to my grandparents in Dover, losing parts of several fingers and a thumb when her hand was crushed in a slammed door. To this day, I shudder whenever children slam doors and usually yell at them to stop. Most recesses at DCD were spent playing capture the flag or other similar games. There were no organized activities such as sports. We had to think up our own. But whenever possible, I was drawn to the pond behind the school to search for frogs, pollywogs, snakes and always hoping there were fish in the pond. There weren't.

My one moment of glory in primary school was playing Good King Wenceslas in the Christmas play. It was a singing part, and I don't actually remember being nervous. Maybe that was simply because I had no idea I couldn't sing very well. I would be very nervous today and may have been, but that memory has faded.

I do recall at least the opening lines of the song, "Good King Wenceslas once looked out on the feast of Stephen, when the snow lay round about, deep and crisp and even."

Perhaps the strongest memory had to do with food, actually the smell from the food. At least once a week, we were served a kind of chicken chop suey. I liked it, but it had a certain smell to it that remained in my sensory system. Even today, if I come across that smell, I am transported instantly back to the dining hall at the school. There are other smells that have the same type of association from different times in my life.

After I left, DCD, I went to Noble and Greenough School, known as Nobles, also in Dedham and not too far from some of my early fishing escapades along the Charles River. Only two of my DCD classmates went to Nobles. One left during the first year and the other dropped back a class. That would have been a better option for me as I was young for my class and was only 17 when I entered college. It is likely that another year would have made me a little more serious about my studies. Re-writing history is the easy part.

It should be noted that in those days, one did not spend a lot of time looking around at schools. At least, I did not and that was true of a lot of my friends. My parents simply said that I was going to Nobles where my father had gone. In fact, the headmaster when I attended the school had been a teacher when my father went there. They were both hard taskmasters, but I managed to ignore their attempted coaching to improve my studies.

The year that I graduated from grade school, I was 11 and my parents had built their new house in Dover on some of the farm property that my maternal grandparents lived on. Moving to Dover and away from Old Farm Rd was a big change for me. I no longer had neighborhood pals to hang around with and I was too young to drive. I'd like to say that I focused on my studies, but that would not be true. I did more things with my cousin, Bob Truesdale, whose family also lived on part of the farm. We only had a short time together since the year after we moved to Dover, he started to go to Middlesex School as a boarder. During the summer, his family went off to Westport, MA and we continued to go to Wareham, MA and Littlejohn Island, ME. However, we were able to cause Bill Morris, the farm manager, at least some heartburn. It was Bob's father, Pie, who had purchased the real go-kart that we raced around the farm roads. A little later in life, he would purchase a Ski-Doo which could zip along at well over 60 mph. It came in handy in the blizzard of 1978 to ride down to Needham to buy groceries or in one case get prescription medication for sick children. Cars had been asked to stay off the roads, but they never mentioned snowmobiles. I even got to pass a police car that was creeping along on the main road. Rte. 128, now Rte. 95 had about 13 miles of cars stranded on the road southbound and abandoned with snow up to the roofs. I rode the Ski-Doo down to the Rte. 109 overpass to view the scene. It was very eerie with the only vehicles moving being the National Guard trucks trying to remove all the cars. It was kind of eerie to watch and took days to clean up.

Bob and I spent some time around the brooks and the ponds, but Bob had yet to catch the fishing bug. Years later, he and I would take his father's Downeast-style power boat, Manitou, about 35 miles offshore and harpoon and land his first swordfish. As we motored in from that adventure, I noticed that the boat would hang tilted in the wrong direction as it passed through the ocean swell. I realized that something had to be causing that. When I opened a hatch in the deck, water was almost to the underside of the deck. There was no electric bilge pump, but there was a standing hand version which took a fair amount of muscle power and effort to work. There was no choice. I started and pumped vigorously. It took a while, but the water level began to go down. I then realized that the engine exhaust pipe was there in the bilge area and if the combination of the cold water and the hot pipe caused it to crack, we would be doomed as the water would likely back into the engine causing it to shut down. That was even more reason to keep at the pump. Bob and I spelled each other and were able to get the water to a reasonable level. Once there, maintenance was easier. Later it was discovered that the stuffing box on the drive shaft had failed, and the water was coming in from there. Another potential disaster avoided. It was without question very exciting to tie up to the dock in Westport, MA with a pretty darn big swordfish on the cockpit deck. This would not be the end of my sword fishing days.

    A few years later, I would be back out to sea in the same area on an 86ft Grand Banks schooner that had been converted for swordfish harpooning. We'll get to that later.

MORE TIME OUTDOORS

I had learned to fly cast by the time that my parents built their house on the farm, and I wanted to fish that way whenever possible. Since I could not legally drive then, it had to be somewhere I could walk or bike. I found out that Noanet and Powissett ponds were stocked with trout by Hale Reservation. The ponds were only a couple of miles through the woods from the Dover house. It required paying for a family fishing membership which I convinced my father was a great idea, then he could join me if he wanted. In the Spring, I would walk up to the ponds at least once a week. The fishing wasn't too bad. Plenty of fish, but no real monsters. I generally released everything. However, when my mother would request one to eat, I'd bring one home for her.

My father was not fond of eating trout, but thought that cod was by far the best fish for eating. He was, however, fond of fly fishing and he had become a member of the Tihonet Club, the scene of my aforementioned adventure in trout fishing that was highlighted with getting hooked by my grandfather. In the spring, we would go to Tihonet quite often to fish. I was always anxious to fish in the Frogfoot reservoir where the biggest trout had been caught over the years and where I would eventually catch a 10 lb rainbow that wasn't the biggest that had been stocked by a member, who had to drain his personal trout pond. The Frogfoot reservoir was perfect trout habitat. It had a cold-water brook running into it and also several springs adding more cool water in the deep areas. It supported some monster snapping turtles as well.

We would also go to the Tihonet area in the fall for upland game hunting. The first time we tried this new adventure was after a morning of duck hunting at Sandham, my father's parents' property. We had our limit of ducks and so my father suggested that we give upland hunting a try around the cranberry bogs of Tihonet.

We had a Labrador retriever by the name of Tosh who was fond of any kind of hunting and retrieving. We tromped around the bogs for a while, and I believe that Tosh had flushed a couple of birds. Most of them we could not get a shot at, but Dad had managed to shoot one. We were separated by a swampy area, and suddenly Tosh flushed two ruffed grouse right in front of me. I took the one going hard left first and then swung back to the other. I saw where the first went down, but so did Tosh and he brought the first bird to me. Then we went to the area where the second went down. I did not have an exact line on it.

As Tosh snuffled around, my father came from behind the swamp and asked if I had hit anything? I told him two grouse. In disbelief, he asked," Are you sure?" Yes was the answer. However Tosh was finding nothing and my looking was fruitless. Finally, Dad said, "It's really unlikely that you shot a double on grouse the first time you hunted them. Most people go an entire lifetime without a double. Let's go." Dejectedly, I started to follow. As I passed the base of a pine tree, I noticed the leaves quivering. I brushed them aside and there was the second bird. I held it up in triumph for my father to see. He smiled and said, "Oh my god!" That was the beginning of a long affair with upland hunting.

The second time we went, I had a double opportunity, but that day I was a mere mortal and mortals miss. Back then grouse were plentiful around the cranberry bog areas. They loved the briar patches for cover and for the berries they produced. There were also occasional coveys of quail and if we got really lucky a pheasant that strayed from Myles Standish Forest where they were stocked.

Unfortunately, the cranberry growers later discovered that the briar patches held bugs that liked to inject their eggs into the cranberries and make them less valuable. So, they cleared all the briars from around the bog areas and shortly thereafter the grouse disappeared.

Rip with a labrador, Tosh, and his double on Ruffed grouse.

A few years earlier when we would have lunch at my maternal grandparents' house in Dover during the winter months, many days there would be 8 or 10 grouse in the bush next to the dining room window eating the berries. Today there are none because the habitat there changed and was not conducive to producing grouse. The grouse in Dover were not hunted, but they were viewed with great curiosity and missed after they were gone.

Some of the habitat changes were directly man-made and others a more natural cycle of pastureland returning to full forest. 150 years ago, 70% of New England was deforested.

For a number of years, I spent most of the summer in Wareham with my grandparents. My parents would come on the weekends and sometimes my mother would stay for a week at a time. Sunday lunches were a big deal and a community affair. My grandmother would go to a local farmstand and buy whatever was in season. Then she'd usually go to Peterson's Ice Cream in Marion and buy chocolate chip and raspberry sherbet. Before lunch, everyone would sit on the porch and participate in shelling peas, cutting beans or shucking corn, depending on what she bought. At lunch, my grandfather would have a tankard or two of ale. The tankard had been given to him and had a glass bottom. He assured us that the glass bottom was so that the person drinking could see if someone was trying to pull a gun on the drinker.

After lunch he would turn on the old black and white tv to the Red Sox baseball game and promptly be snoring away. I found it amazing that without fail, he could give you the games score and who got the hits. I always thought there had to be some trick, but never found out.

While Grandad had an almost perfect knowledge of baseball, I always questioned if he really knew the names of all his grandchildren. If he wanted me to do something, he rarely ever used my name. Perhaps that was a leftover from the surgical ward. I do know that he was considered to have been very generous with his surgical talent. He operated on and saved a number of patients who had no money to pay him. Some made money later in life and paid him handsomely then. One amazing token of payment was in his summer tackle room. A patient whose life he saved had only minimal use of deformed hands and with those and his feet he built my grandfather a beautiful model of a sailing ship complete with rigging and detailed painting. I doubt that I could have done anything close to it with both functional hands.

Dr. J H Cunningham's pewter tankard
with his initials and "auld lang syne" inscribed.

   It was in this tackle room that numerous fly-fishing strategy sessions were held by the "Generals" consisting of my grandfather, father, and various fishing partners. As a mere foot soldier, I picked up bits and pieces of the conversations about outsmarting the monster trout in Tihonet's Frogfoot reservoir. This talk was a mysterious and magical happening in the tackle room. A place that I was not allowed unattended, but a place I frequented when no one was looking. It was a room that could keep a kid poking endlessly through draws, jars, and into corners stacked deep with equipment. I began to examine snelled flies and leaders and to marvel that these weird creations actually caught fish. The desire to know more began to grow. When I was too young to operate motorboat, I would paddle a dingy around in the cove in front of the Wareham house and catch blue crabs. My grandfather would pay a nickel apiece. If, however, I could find a soft-shelled crab, that was worth a quarter! I would also walk out to the beach and dig soft-shelled clams and find quahogs. I would also get some money for supplying those to my grandfather.

Dr. John H Cunningham (grandfather) fishing off his catboat.

Later on, I did not have a formal summer job, but would make a few dollars doing odd jobs around the property or over at my grandmother's sister's house just down the dirt road. Their place was where my father's boat was moored and where I was able to keep the skiff with a 25 hp outboard that my father bought for me to use. After that happened, I got into a routine of fishing early in the mornings and late in the evenings for striped bass. Back in those days anyone could catch and sell fish without any sort of permit. So that kept me busy. Doing what I liked and making a little money at it, what's not to like. My biggest problem was finding someone who would drive me to the fish market in Buzzards Bay to sell my catch. When I fished for pure fun, I'd wade the sand flats out in front of the house and catch striped bass on a fly rod. All of this was an unplanned foundation to what I'd do later in life.

Granddad Cunningham with a caught shark.

At the end of each summer, it was back to school at Nobles and hitting the books. I take full responsibility for my failure to really apply myself during high school. But certainly, I was not focused on learning. I played football in the Fall, played what was called social hockey in the winter and rowed on the crew in the spring. My senior year, I was the captain of the crew and while not winning the New England Interscholastic Rowing Association (NEIRA) championship at Lake Quinsigamond, we had a very good year.

Author, second from left,
racing on the Charles River at Nobles.

My studies were poor enough that my parents decided that I should be a boarding student my senior year and then I could not skip the evening study halls. The concept was good, but I still had some distractions in the form of friends. Actually, the distractions were mostly after study hall when we had some time in the dorm before we would have mandatory lights out. I was like most teenagers for whom food was a big deal. Most of the boarders were in what was called "the castle," since it was built like one and looked like one. That also housed the kitchen and dining facilities for all the students.

We liked to have a snack before bedtime, but bringing your own food was frowned upon and so were any appliances to cook on. A former fellow student, Dan Ingalls, who was wicked smart, invented the Ingalls' hot dog cooker. It was two tenpenny nails and an old extension cord. The wall plug was left on, and the other end was removed. The wires were stripped and wrapped one on each nail. If you had electrical tape that would keep the wiring in place and making good contact. Then all you needed was a hot dog. The nails were inserted about an inch in each end of the hot dog then rested on a plate not held in the hand and the plug was plugged in. The lights in the castle would dim slightly and 10 seconds later your dog was steaming hot. Ingenious. The next problem was a good source of hot dogs. Through a little trial and error, we discovered that the kitchen freezer which held all kinds of food, but was locked, could be opened by a sharp upward pull on the handle. So, we'd grab a few dogs and then began a little business of selling hot dogs to other boarding students.

I lived in the Round Room, which was in one of the round turrets that gave the castle its distinctive look, with 3 other classmates, Dick Harwood, Harry Stimpson and Bill Colby. Harry had a father who ran for US Congress, so we had a few campaign signs in the room. Then Harry, being a dutiful son, would remove his father's opponent's signs and for some reason brought them to our room. After a short while there were quite a number and the dorm master, who lived on the same floor, told us to remove them all. We got a big trash can that was on wheels and began to fill it up. When it appeared to be full, I sat on top to squash everything down. My roommates proceeded to push me down in so that my arms and legs were sticking straight up. I was stuck. Then they rolled me down the hall at a good rate and I banged into the dorm master's door. He opened it up and shouted that I should get out immediately. "Yes sir," I responded, "I would if I could, but I can't." Did he help me? No. He rolled me back to our dorm room where my three roommates were miraculously in bed with the lights turned out. It took a little while, but I got removed and so did all the signs and my roommates had a good laugh.

For most of my senior year, my final junior year report card was taped to the mirror in my bathroom at home. I was told to leave it there by my father. Mr. Putnam, the Headmaster, had written in bold letters, "Colin will not go to college unless there is dramatic improvement." Prophetic, but not correct.

I did graduate, but my options to go to a New England college were restricted by my lack of good grades and by my poor performance on the SAT's (Scholastic Aptitude Tests). Once again, I picked a college sight unseen, but my choices were few and luckily I happened to pick the right one.

III

MATURER OUTLETS

JOHN H CUNNINGHAM

As we grew older, we automatically put aside certain activities which had kept our parents and the neighborhood from sleeping nights, as too juvenile to be continued. Other methods of expressing our joy in living took their place. Theatrical performances, naturally, came into our program. The first show in which George Cohan, one of America's greatest actors, playwrights, and producers, took part, was given in my cellar. The price of admission was ten pins or their equivalent. We had a large audience, which sat around on boxes, saw-horses, and on the cellar-stairs. A bedsheet was used as curtain, and the coal-bin served as entrance and exit for the actors. In this show, which was rather a Wild West performance, George was the villain and I the hero, this arrangement being made because it was my house, which gave me the choice of parts.

During the morning, prior to the matinee, George and the rest of us went to the brickyard, back of Powder Horn Hill, and collected some red brick-dust from around the ovens. At the point in the play where the hero was supposed to dispose of the villain, George had this brick-dust mixed with water in a paper bag hanging around his neck under his white shirt. At the proper moment I leaped out of the coal-bin, attacked him with the bread-knife, and struck him skillfully with the handle rather than the blade, thus breaking the bag. This permitted the red concoction of water and brick-dust to flow freely, staining the villain's shirt in a most realistic manner. We had been so generous with our gory fluid that it not only soaked George's shirt but practically submerged him. George's acting was excellent even as a boy, and the whole skit was so realistic that the frightened children stampeded, leaving us no audience for the rest of the show. As we were cleaning up, many of the kids peeked in through the cellar-windows, and some of the braver ones ventured back. It was through them that the more frightened ones were made to realize that the villain had not really been murdered. It simply became necessary to take him upstairs, wash out the stains, and dry his clothes before he dared go home.

George was one of a famous family of four, which, as "The Four Cohans," went on the stage when he was quite young. Their first performance, I believe, was given on Chelsea Marsh, in a tent. Later, this family combination went on the vaudeville circuit, and my playmate began to write patriotic musical comedies. Later still he became a manager, and now owns a theater in New York which is called by his name.

George also played on our ball-team, but was a poor player because he could not keep his mind on the game. He was always instinctively practicing dancing steps, the mastery of which afterwards made him famous. Rhythm and humming songs were a part of his every action. If there is anything in the theory of beginning early and sticking to one thing to achieve success, Cohan offers a good example.

On this same ball-team there were other notable characters: Charlie Mitchell, later a noted banker; Billy Robinson, one of "Our Gang," became famous not only in football and baseball, but also as the holder of the amateur 300-yard indoor record. We also claimed as one of us Piggy Oldredge, who was the first person to invent "water-boots" with which he could walk on the surface of the water. The "Professor," as he came to be called, used to perform at picnics, where he would undertake to walk half the distance on the water that some athlete, in the same time, would require to run along the beach. He also made trips from Revere Beach around Boston Light. On an attempt to walk from Boston to New York he met with mishaps, and almost lost his life.

Even Tragedy was represented on our team. One of our members, Trefethern, was later accused of murder. The story was that, as a climax of some emotional affair, he threw his lady-love, Tena Davis, off Mystic River Bridge, near the Cochrane Chemical Works (now the Monsanto Chemical Plant). The tide was out, and she landed on her head in the mud and was killed. Fortunately, our friend was acquitted, so he probably was not a murderer after all, although suspicion continued in spite of the favorable verdict. Another member of the team, Steve Mahoney, became one of the best light-weight professional boxers, and is now the head of the sporting department of one of our largest newspapers.

WHEN I was a boy, private schools were limited in number, and all the children of our community went to the Carter Grammar School. The teachers were known as "biddies," and any misdemeanor by a pupil was punished by taking the culprit into the cap-room and giving him a predetermined number of strokes with a rattan on his extended hand. If, for any reason, the hand was withdrawn, the rattan was applied to the legs until the hand was again extended and had received the number of strokes which the misdemeanor demanded. The schedule of the number of strokes for the various "crimes" was well known to the boys.

On the corner of the street, near the school, there was the usual small store where the boys congregated and bought the various things that kids enjoy. This store was kept by an old Scotchman, who was the boys' best friend; but he was typical of his race. He usually had the price attached to each article. On one occasion, while I was in the store buying some apples, on a pile of which was a sign "two for a cent," the most unpopular teacher in the school came in. In those days women were dressed in full skirts and bustles, the latter consisting of wire cages something like a big baseball mask, attached to their posteriors, beneath the skirt, thus forming an enormous hump at the rear. The particular bustle worn by this teacher seemed to me just the proper place on which to attach the sign, "Two for a cent." I accomplished the deed without the teacher's knowledge, and she went up the street, passing among the various children who were playing about before school.

Children do not miss much, and the sign was soon discovered. There was a good deal of giggling, and many remarks were passed. The teacher soon discovered that something was amiss. Her pet (there were always such in our classes) supplied her with the necessary information. She realized that the sign must have come from the Scotchman's store, and holding it in her hand, she returned and made her indignant protest. The old Scotchman, always fair and lacking in appreciation of this type of humor, offered a reward of $1.00 for anyone who would tell him who played the trick, threatening arrest for the culprit.

Needless to say, there are always tattle-tales in a school, and the storekeeper was soon informed that I was the guilty party. When I heard that I had been discovered, I went in to see him and confessed my crime. When I explained that I did it just as a joke, he asked me a good many questions. Then, much to my surprise, instead of promptly turning me over to the police, he told me to come back the next day and he would have me arrested then. I went in the following day as agreed, but he said that I had such an innocent face he really couldn't bear to see me behind the bars. This was one of the many times that I was glad I was my mother's child!

FIGHTING among boys at school is a form of athletics that now seems practically obsolete, but it was a common thing in my day. If a quarrel started before school it was settled after that day's session on Powder Horn Hill, now the site of the Soldiers' Home, Chelsea. When a fight was on, there was much anticipation during school-hours. As soon as we were let out, the leader of the boys, surrounded by all interested, would wait for the contestants. Occasionally a boy would be cowardly and sneak away, but this seldom happened. It would be bad news for such a boy, as he could never live down such action.

As the young fighters joined the waiting crowd, they would usually glare at each other and start to climb the hill to the arena - a ring about ten feet in diameter formed by a circle of sods. The excitement of such an occasion cannot be described and is only appreciated by those who have actually been participants. Perhaps the expressions of emotion on the faces of the accompanying boys was hardly less intense. A dead silence ensued, and an atmosphere of serious intent - something like "going over the top." Some of the fights were real scraps, as the unwritten rules required that the contestants should continue until one gave in. The spirit of a boy is not easily broken, and the punishment that the pugnacious youngsters received was sometimes severe.

Out of all this, several outstanding scrappers were developed in the school, and there were some who afterwards became professionally prominent. We had a real incentive to become proficient in fighting, as John L. Sullivan and Jim Godfrey, the famous colored pugilist, used to train in the vicinity; and these characters were objects of great interest to all the boys who were not sissies.

Young George Godfrey, son of Jim Godfrey just mentioned, and Sandy Ferguson, the "Chelsea bad boy," who, through deviltry, threw away a good chance to become the world's heavyweight champion, were members of my class, and gained their early training in contests in the ring on Powder Horn Hill.

Everyone interested in the fight-game knows the remarkable history of John L. Sullivan. Unfortunately for him, when he was in his prime Mr. Volstead had never been heard of, and it was not an uncommon thing for the famous John to go on a spree. When this happened, John L. was something to be avoided. We boys, seeing him staggering down the street, always knew that there would be something doing, so a procession usually followed behind at a safe distance. Frequently, when the famous pugilist met somebody coming from the other direction on the sidewalk, he would sail into him without provocation. Policemen had a horror of him, and when he went on one of his sprees he usually had a clear road. But when in training, and not drinking, John L. was one of the most kindly souls in the world. Some of us boys were privileged to go to his training quarters at Revere Beach and admire the gladiator in his workouts. His position in regard to drinking in his later life, when he became a temperance advocate, makes great reading, as he had a manner of expression which was not only forceful but unique in the construction of the language. A book published a few years ago by Dibble, "The Life of John L. Sullivan," will do no boy harm to read.

THE advent of bicycles was an event which created great general interest. The first were those curiously contrived vehicles known as the high wheel. There was a large front-wheel, approximately five or six feet in diameter, on which the pedals were located, and a saddle, just behind the center, attached to a metal tube running backwards, to which was attached a small wheel about two feet in diameter. As the center of gravity was almost in the center of the big wheel, riding down an incline required leaning backward to keep from taking a header. If the rider did not steer clear of fair-sized rocks, or preserve a proper balance, he would pitch forward over the large front-wheel. These "headers" were of common occurrence.

A favorite stunt was to put one's legs over the handle-bars, and coast down steep hills. This was extremely dangerous and resulted in many accidents. Some inventor, to overcome this, devised a bicycle with the small wheel in front. This, however, never became popular because it lacked the speed, and perhaps the danger associated with the high wheel. Another inventor secured propulsion by substituting levers with a strap on the large-wheel hub, so that up-and-down motions of treading propelled the machine. This bicycle was called the "Star."

If I am not mistaken, the first safety-bicycle came into existence about 1890. The tires were of solid rubber, and the machine cost $125, so that only boys with so-called "rich" parents could afford one. The famous Linscott Road Race started at the Stone House on Everett Avenue (still standing on the Revere Beach Boulevard). The route was to Spy Pond and back, a distance of about twenty-five miles.

The Linscott Road Race was the first, I believe, in this country, and developed some of the greatest bicycle-riders in the history of the game. Notable among them was Jimmy Moran, commonly called "Piggy." This nickname came from the fact that his father kept a lot of pigs, and Jimmy used to collect the neighborhood garbage. The first machine that Jimmy ever had was an old one of mine, which I gave him. He became perhaps the best-known six-day bicycle-rider in America, and was among the greatest of all distance-riders, being the world's champion for a long period of time.

The first pneumatic-tire safety-bicycle, I believe, was made by Peter Berlow, a professional skater, and a mechanic by trade. He turned up at one of the Linscott Road Races with his bicycle equipped with large tubes, inflated with air, and bound onto the frame of the wheel by elastic tape. Evidently this gave increased speed to the bicycle, and when Peter had got about half-way back from Spy Pond on the return trip, he was miles in the lead. Unfortunately, the tape, which was bound around the tire as well as the rim, wore out, and the tires came off. Whether or not this pneumatic tire was original with Pete I don't know, but it was not long afterward that it became standard bicycle equipment. Air-cushion tires (about one inch in circumference, and filled with air, but which could not be inflated with a pump) and the pneumatic-tire (which was larger and could be inflated with air) came into general use.

The safety-bicycle grew in popularity, and road races were contests which attracted much attention. The riders used to represent different bicycle concerns, and the best riders were, therefore, used for house-publicity through participating in these contests. One of the most important events was the Century Run, which started from Chelsea Square and went over the Newburyport Turnpike to Newburyport and back, a distance of about a hundred miles.

Interest in bicycling ran high. On Sunday mornings and holidays, I used to join a group of these semiprofessionals, including the McLean brothers (one of whom, Aleck, afterwards became a noted prizefighting manager and took Jack Johnson on his famous Australian and European tour), the McDuffy boys, Jimmy Moran, and a lot of others. We would start from Chelsea Square and ride out to the Brookline Reservoir, where we would spend the day. The Reservoir furnished a very satisfactory bicycle-track, the distance around one of the reservoirs being about a mile and a half. There was much gambling in connection with these affairs, and professional bookmakers used to sell tickets on the events. Riding from Chelsea to the Reservoir, a distance of about twelve miles, having several races, and then riding home, made quite a day of exercise. We did not consider it such a great stunt in those days, but with the present-day tendency toward limited physical effort, it would seem that boys of my time must have been much hardier than they are today.

ATHLETIC events were among our chief interests in those days. Boxing was part of a boy's daily routine, and all the real boys seemed to enjoy it. This event was usually staged in the cellars of our houses, and occasionally out of doors. As my father was enthusiastic about athletic exercise, the gymnasium which he fitted up for me (as well as for himself) at the top of our house was the place where the more important boxing matches took place. Here we had all the "fixin's." While there was no ring, there was a ten-foot square marked on the floor. We had no ropes, but did have buckets, sponges, and stools to rest on between rounds.

One of the events that I recall was a contest between Dana Evans and myself. While we usually stripped to the waist, on this occasion we kept our shirts on and our sleeves down. During the contest the button on the cuff of my shirt ripped a six-inch gash in Dana's forearm which necessitated taking him to the Doctor, where the wound had to be sewed up with several stitches. This accident made it quite an event.

My father gave me lessons in the manly art and used me quite rough at times. While he was able to get little practice, I was at it almost daily. The end of Father's career as a boxer occurred when he took me into the gymnasium one evening, and much to his surprise and mine, I knocked him out. I could never induce him to put on the gloves again. He did not entirely lose his interest and continued to take me with him to professional boxing-contests. Thus, I had the privilege of seeing John L. Sullivan and the famous wrestler, Muldoon, give an exhibition of boxing, wrestling, and living-pictures at the Academy of Music. I also went with Father to Music Hall, now Loew's Orpheum, where I saw some of the pugilistic notables of that time, including Jake Kilrain, Paddy Ryan, George Dixon, and the Belfast Spider.

In connection with the boxing-game, I remember how interested we boys were in the contest between John L. Sullivan and Jim Corbett, in September 1892. On the day of that event, I was attending a performance at the old Boston Museum, on Tremont Street near Scollay Square, in which the famous wax-figures were exhibited. After leaving the theater, the bells were ringing all over the city, and we heard the incredible news that the great Sullivan had been knocked out by Corbett, and a new champion had been crowned.

WHEN we boys had saved up enough money to go to the theater, we seldom had enough left to pay five cents for a ride on the horse-cars from Chelsea to Boston. We usually attended a Saturday matinee, there being no school on that day, and we used to start from home early and walk over, go to Faneuil Hall Market, buy some cheese (which was then eight cents a pound), and, with a few crackers, have our lunch. Thus, we were among the first who went up into "cheap heaven," which was the part of the theater where we could afford to buy tickets.

The first show that I remember seeing was at the Howard Athenaeum, now the Old Howard. It had previously been a church (which seems ironical in view of the present performances), and the only change that had been made in the appearance of the church was the stage, which occupied the place where the pulpit had been. Frank Harris accompanied me on this occasion, and the play was "Kit, the Arkansas Traveler." The legitimate Howard Theater later was turned into a vaudeville house, and the performances became rather athletic in character, featuring noted fighters, wrestlers, and acrobats.

On one occasion, when we were fortunate enough to have floor-seats on the aisle directly beneath the gallery, a man, very drunk, fell out of the balcony, and, just missing me, landed in the aisle. Much to our surprise, he got up without assistance, not being hurt in the least.

An outstanding theatrical performance, called "The Corsican Brothers," to which Frank also accompanied me, was at the new Bowdoin Square Theater in the same district, located directly opposite the Revere House, which was then the finest hotel in Boston. Here had been entertained Royalty on the few occasions that New England was favored by such personages. Frank and I had seats in the balcony, the price of which, I remember, was twenty-five cents each. This was more than we usually paid, as we could go in cheap heaven for ten cents. Frank became very much excited over the play, and when the villain was attacked by the hero, he stood up and yelled, "Give it to him," adding other expressions of approval that the villain was receiving his due at last. This resulted in our getting into trouble with the ushers. While Frank really intended to behave, his excitement was such that he could not control himself. After further exclamations at the top of his voice, we were summarily expelled.

Aside from the Howard, the Bowdoin Square, and the Boston Museum, there were few places of amusement in Boston at that time. On one occasion Father took me to a matinee at the Boston Museum, but I have forgotten the name of the show. I recollect that afterwards we went across the street to Clair's Restaurant, which, in those days, was quite the most select place in the city. Old Clair took great pride in his food. He had only ten tables or so. If one wished to dine there, he would have to drop in and tell Mr. Clair when to expect him, and also express his preference in the matter of food.

CLAIR was famous for his game, ducks, and fish. It was a great privilege to go there with Father, who also had one of his friends for dinner. The thing that surprised me, and which has always reminded me of the place, was associated with the selection of cigars after dinner. Clair presented his guests with several boxes from which to choose, and Father's friend took cigars from several of the boxes and felt them over carefully. He and Clair became involved in a long discussion about the rolling of the cigars, the guest insisting that they were too loose. This upset Mr. Clair very much, as he felt that the cigars, like the food he served, represented the last word. The argument that followed alarmed me. I presume it was all friendly enough, but the discussion became so heated that I fully expected to see a fight.

Another restaurant on Tremont Street was Copeland's. This was located opposite the junction of Park and Tremont Streets, where the store of R.H. Stearns Company now stands. This restaurant was rather a resort for the ladies and the more refined men. The floor was laid in large white-and-black, octagonal shaped marbled tiles, and the chairs were of filigreed iron construction. The tables were also in this same design, with marble tops. The walls were painted white, and there was considerable gilt about. The general appearance was more that of a modern French restaurant than anything else.

As one thinks of Clair's and Copeland's it brings back a remembrance of Taft's Hotel, which was in Winthrop, located on the beach at a point where Shirley Gut runs through. This place, like Clair's, was one of the noted eating-places. Father used to take me down there occasionally for lunch on Sunday, and I believe Point Shirley was the first place where I ever dug clams. We used to drive down in the Goddard buggy with old Kate, who was quite a fine mare, and while Father was in the hotel I would go down on the beach to watch the men dig clams. Naturally, I became interested, and, while I had no fork, I dug a good many with my hands. These clams, I remember distinctly, Father had specially cooked, although there were probably not very many; but he wished to encourage my enterprise as a reward for industry.

Taft had a room which had an ice-chest in the form of a showcase, in which he kept his fish, game, and meats. Also terrapin, the first I had ever seen. The procedure was quite a ceremony. Taft would carefully scrutinize what he had to serve and would then pick out the particular delicacies his guests desired. In talking the matter over with older gentlemen in recent times, I learned that I evidently missed Taft's wine cellar, which was very famous. I presume Father was inspecting this while I was digging clams.

The excursions to Taft's were always great events to me. On the Sundays when Father did not take me there, he sometimes had old Kate hitched up, and, with two empty, five-gallon stone jugs, we would go to Everett Spring, which was only about a mile or two from our house. The water from this spring was famous for its purity. The spring itself was housed in a rather small, wooden building, and as an enterprise proved very profitable. The Company had a few teams with large, wooden tanks, somewhat resembling sprinkling-carts. These had a route through the various neighborhoods, and the spring-water was sold at one cent a gallon. Father preferred to get his own supply or send directly to the spring for it, rather than take it from the wooden tanks, as he felt these were perhaps not sanitary. In passing, I may say that "sanitary" was a word I never heard in childhood, although now it seems to be associated with everything!

A GREAT event of my childhood occurred while Father and Mother were on a winter trip in Florida. My grandmother, who used to live in Charlestown, usually came to take charge of the house during their absence. Grandmother was very severe in watching over our deportment, especially at the table, and had the old-fashioned idea that we should never take on our plates more than we could eat, and that whatever was provided had to be accepted without comment. Often there would be things that my sister and I did not care for, and we used to deposit them, at opportune moments when Grandmother was not paying attention to us, on the sill under the table. When the meal was finished, we usually disposed of our discards in one way or another, but occasionally our dog, who was often in the dining-room, had his eye on us, and he would get under the table and eat up what we had hidden, thus saving us further trouble.

Grandmother was not very keen on the dog, and finally he gave our trick away. We both received adequate punishment when the old lady found out what we had been doing. Whether or not her conscience hurt her for having punished us too severely, I do not know, but she afterwards bought me a balloon attached to a red stick, which, with a rubber-band stretched over the end, made a toy that afforded great pleasure. By blowing on the stick the balloon filled up, and, as the air escaped by the rubber-reed, it would give out a prolonged squeak.

These toys were quite common and were greatly prized. We boys had an idea that if we sucked the collapsed rubber-balloon it could then be brought to greater inflation. While I was demonstrating this, one day, it slipped down my throat, wooden flute and all. The idea of having a balloon inside me frightened Grandmother out of her wits, and, in spite of the Doctor's assurance that the object would probably pass through me, she became so panicky that she telegraphed Father and Mother to return immediately from Florida. I was a bit worried myself, as I feared that in taking a deep breath the balloon would blow up and start squeaking. Somehow this did not occur. The Doctor was correct in his expectations, and the balloon was duly passed, but not until Father and Mother had started on their trip home, presumably to attend my funeral.

While Grandmother possessed very little sense of humor, our old nurse, Kate Casey, had a liberal supply. When Father and Mother came into the front hall, very much excited, I allayed their apprehension by meeting them. Mother immediately asked if we had recovered the balloon, and Kate and I took great satisfaction in pointing to it, inflated and with a ribbon tied around it, floating in all its glory from the hall chandelier.

The only other unusual object that I remember swallowing was what we used to call a minstrel ring. This was a large piece of cut-glass, mounted like a diamond, on a ring, to be worn on the finger. It was an object which graced the hands of members of most of the minstrel troupes of that day. This likewise passed and was added to the balloon collection, which Mother kept in her possession for years.

MY FATHER was active in establishing the Plymouth and Kingston Street Railway. This was the first electric line in that section of the country and ran from Kingston to Chiltonville. The outing that people seemed to enjoy most, at that time, was taking trolley-rides. To further this interest, the Hotel Pilgrim, which was a distance of about three miles from the center of Plymouth, was purchased by the Road, and a trolley line was run out to it. My family became established in this hotel during the Summer, and Father, during the evening, could keep his eye on the development of the Road's activities. There was a bar in the basement of this hotel, which was well patronized, and band concerts and other amusements were given at the hotel to induce people to use the trolleys. All this opened up a new vista for my activities.

Jack Burke, the bar-tender, did a flourishing business in the basement, and was a great friend of us boys. Malcolm Whitman, who afterwards became the world's tennis champion, and I, were constant companions, and when we were not playing tennis, we were very likely to be found fishing in the pond or in the bay nearby. Trapping skunks was another of our chief pastimes. On one occasion, when we had captured a skunk in a boxtrap, we thought it would be amusing to play a trick on bar-tender Jack. We transferred the skunk from the trap into an empty barrel that stood in the corner of the bar-room. We covered the top of the barrel with a table-cloth. At first the skunk accommodated by giving off its odor so that the bar-room was saturated, yet nobody could seem to find the point from which the smell originated.

Then, it seemed to us, the skunk laid down on his job. During the evening, while there was a large gathering enjoying refreshments, Malcolm and I slipped into the room and, with a broom-handle, jabbed the skunk until he resumed operations. The stench drove everybody out of the room. Jack got on to what we had done, and, catching us, locked us up in the bar-room with the skunk, thus making the punishment fit the crime. He told us we were to stay there until we had killed the skunk and were ready to dispose of it. This furnished a new phase to our escapade. The skunk was finally killed, but not until Malcolm and I were thoroughly saturated. We both decided that this was an indoor sport scarcely worth continuing.

EXCURSIONS to the shipyards along the Mystic River furnished one of my chief pleasures. Buck's Lumber Yard was one of the favorite places. On one occasion I was dared by a companion to go up the rope-ladder to the crosstree of the mainmast of a schooner unloading along side of the wharf. Of course, I did it, but, when I got up there and realized the height, I became frightened, and did not dare to come down. Some men on the wharf, seeing me there, insisted upon my immediate descent. Their orders, however, were not promptly obeyed, due entirely to fear. I think this was the first time that I ever knew what fear was, and, strange as it may seem, the fear of height has always remained.

There are two outstanding instances, which occurred in later life, that make me believe that this complex must have been born at that time. One instance was an occasion on which Jack Chamberlin and I sailed a canoe from Manomet, South Plymouth, to Duxbury, making a visit to the Miles Standish Monument. The monument at that time was not finished inside, and in order to gain the top one had to go up a ladder to a plank from which another ladder ran, and thus finally reach the top. Everything was wonderful until it came time to descend, when I looked down the inside of the shaft. A vivid appreciation of the fact that it was a long drop, and that the ladders were rather rickety, placed a great load on my self-control in making the descent.

The other occasion was while I was sheep-hunting in lower California with John Phillips, on an expedition which he had organized to secure specimens for the Agassiz Museum at Harvard of a new species of sheep which had recently been discovered there. I was alone, and trying to get to sheep on another mountain, when I unexpectedly found myself on a narrow ridge about a foot in width, with a drop of a few thousand feet on either side. Fear suddenly possessed me, and I straddled the ridge. Here again it was only by the realization that I simply had to get off that I finally forced myself to make the attempt and overcame the impulse to jump. It seems paradoxical that, with this fear, I can walk a long distance on a railroad track with excellent balance, yet cannot go on a much wider walk if it is at a height. I became subject to this obsession during my first trip to Niagara Falls, where I felt an almost irresistible impulse to jump in.

AROUND Plymouth there were a good many old sea captains and others who had followed the sea, by whom I was greatly impressed. As I became interested in the sea, and talked with Mother about it, I found that her father had been a sea-captain and her three brothers had likewise followed the sea. The name of one of them, Nathaniel Prouty, is still to be found in the roster of Dana's "Two Years Before the Mast," in which my uncle is put down as the "Scituate Boy, Able Seaman." All this and many other narratives gave me an almost irresistible desire to emulate my sailor friends in some way. I talked the matter over with my boy friends, and the only one interested was Billy Robinson, with whom I had already had so many ad ventures. Acting on my suggestion, he discovered that we could get a job on one of the cattle-ships, which at that time were running frequently from Charles town to Liverpool. For many years Charlestown was the place where cattle from the West were loaded on these steamers under the supervision of a Doctor Bryden, who served as inspector of cattle for that district. Billy knew Doctor Bryden, and through him learned that men and sometimes boys were signed up for each boat, at an office located at the lower end of State Street, to take care of the cattle on the way over. The remuneration was small, but one got his food and an opportunity, without work, to look about while the ship was being unloaded on the other side.

Billy and I made up our minds to make this trip without our parents knowing anything about it, as we both felt certain that they would not permit it. We walked over from Chelsea one Saturday at the beginning of our summer vacation, found the office, and signed up on a boat which was to leave two days later. Whether or not Billy talked in his sleep, or how it came to pass, I never knew; but his father learned of our intention, came to see my father, and exposed the whole affair. Billy's father was willing that his son should go, but mine was obdurate. That was troublesome, but not necessarily final.

Billy and I had a conference, and we arranged that he was to come around to my house about four in the morning on the day we were to sail, that I would sneak out and join him, and that we would make the trip and take the consequences. The first part of the plan worked perfectly. Billy showed up under my bedroom window, gave the signal, and I, being very much awake waiting for him and already to go, got up and dressed. Then I found to my chagrin that my bedroom door had been locked by my too-understanding father! This added to the difficulty, but I threw my small package of luggage out of the window, and, swinging onto the water-spout, crawled down. As I was almost at the bottom, Father opened the back door and greeted me. Billy, standing nearby, ran away, and Father took me back into the house and locked me in a closet. Here I remained until the boat had sailed. Billy joined the ship, and upon his return related his adventures. It has always been one of the tragedies of my life that I could not have made that trip with him.

My uncle, Nathaniel Prouty, followed the sea for many years after his trip with Dana. I know very few of the details of his career, but I recollect one story about his being on a square-rigged ship, bound for New Bedford, loaded presumably with some inflammable cargo. The ship got on fire while Uncle Nat was asleep, and was abandoned, the rest of the crew leaving Nat, then a boy of about twenty, behind, evidently forgotten in the confusion. Whether or not Uncle Nat put the fire out, or whatever came to pass, the ship was not destroyed, and the boy was faced with the problem of salvaging her. I have seen newspaper clippings from Boston and New Bedford papers describing how he single-handedly, maneuvered this ship with her cargo to port. He was given a large sum of money by the ship-owners and was promoted to be captain of one of the other ships belonging to this company.

DURING my youth there seemed to be a general feeling among my companions that association with girls was a "sissy" trait, and we looked upon those boys who seemed to enjoy going to parties as far beneath our consideration. Naturally we had to go to certain girls' birthday parties, but we always felt that they were ordeals. We usually contrived, in some way or other, to do something to demonstrate our superiority over those boys who took pleasure in such social experiences. It should be admitted, however, that each of us had a secret interest in some girl, but so secret that we guarded against its discovery by the others.

Even in those days mothers thought that dancing school was part of a boy's education. My old nurse, Kate Casey, recalls that I rebelled and insists that when only eight years of age I made a remark, which I would like to doubt, that "girls were not my nature." However, I was regularly dressed up each week and deposited among the other Lord Fauntleroys and dolled-up girls. On one occasion I made my escape. Somehow I secured a bright-red, elastic, slate-cover, a device which was stretched around the wooden frame of a school slate, to prevent noise. This I adjusted about my forehead, and then, yelling in apparent distress, rushed into the garden where my mother was sitting. Of course, Mother thought I had had my head split open, and was greatly alarmed until she discovered my trick. I had accomplished my object of getting out of dancing school for that day, but when Father returned and gave me a good licking I was not sure that my strategy had been wholly successful.

I recollect an early personal interest in the sister of one of my friends who was not in Our Gang. Sometimes I would visit this friend's house on the pretense of seeing him, but in reality to have the enjoyment of seeing the sister. She and I became good friends, and when it became necessary to invite some young lady to a social event, she was usually my choice. My sister, I believe, was the only one who suspected my sentiments, and, knowing my feeling in regard to girls in general, missed no opportunity to make fun of me, which was exactly what I dreaded. I always referred to this young lady as the "Venus de

Prattsville," the idea being born of my sister's reference to her resemblance to the statue of Venus de Milo which I had in my room - which statue I have always admired.

One day in the Winter this girl asked me if I would drive with her in her sleigh to visit a relative who lived some five or six miles in the country. It happened that I could do this without any of the boys getting onto it, so I accepted. We left early one Saturday morning in a two-seated sleigh, all tucked in with a big buffalo robe and a very spirited horse which she asked me to drive. We started off bravely, and I took good care to select the back roads so that none of my friends should see me in such a compromising situation. I can recollect nothing regarding our topics of conversation, but I still remember my embarrassment at being alone with a girl for whom I had a peculiar, yet I presume normal sentiment.

The horse apparently had not been out of the stable for some time and was feeling particularly gay. His desire to go fast of course relieved my embarrassment, as I had to pay much attention to him, and, on the whole, his behavior gave me pleasure. We had gone some few miles on our journey when the horse broke into a run, and soon I realized that we were involved in a real runaway. The horse took us off the road and into a large field. The sleigh was first on one runner and then on the other. Finally, striking a snowbank, the sleigh was upset, throwing us out, while the horse continued merrily on his way. The last we saw of him he was disappearing in some woods, where there was no road.

Here I was, left alone with a girl in a snowbank - a situation that scarcely lessened my embarrassment! Her attitude, being that of amusement rather than fear, increased my high appreciation of her. We finally got straightened out, and, proceeding in the direction in which the horse had disappeared, we found parts of the sleigh which had been completely destroyed by hitting the trees as the horse went through the grove into which he had run. The horse was later recovered, and, when we explained our experience to the girl's family, there was a little lifting of the eyebrows on the part of her mother, which indicated to me that she was not inclined to look too seriously upon our escapade.

I must admit that my appreciation of this girl's qualities increased as time went on, and I took opportunities to be in her society more openly. Somehow, she seemed to be interested in adventuresome activities more than other girls, and we always seemed to be getting into some sort of difficulty together. On one occasion, during the Summer, I accepted an invitation to visit her family at the seashore, and she and I started off in a rowboat for the purpose of fishing on a ledge two or three miles' distance from the shore. While we were enjoying fair fishing, the sea gradually became rougher. Finally, it got so rough that, when we started to return, the water kept breaking into the boat, and it became evident that we were going to swamp. Realizing this, and noticing a bell buoy in the vicinity, we made for it. When we reached it the boat was nearly filled with water. We both got out on the bell buoy and fastened the boat to one of the uprights. Neither of us was frightened, and, holding onto the iron structure that suspended the bell, which was making plenty of noise in the rough sea, we thought we were having a great lark. We were both soaking wet, and had we been inclined to seasickness we had every condition that would contribute to it. However, after enjoying our situation for about an hour, a boat came to our rescue, as we had been spotted by someone on the shore.

Such experiences as this and the sleigh-ride naturally had the e.ff ect of cementing our friendship. When I went to college, at which time it was the custom for girls to make sofa pillows to help furnish our rooms, she sent me a very large one with a knitted bell-buoy on it. Unbeknownst to everybody, this was one of my proud possessions!

A year or two later I accepted an invitation to go to her family's home at the beach for dinner and arrived there by train. I had not been invited to spend the night and intended to take the last train back to Boston; but the moonlight, enthusiasm, or what-not, prevented my arriving at the station until after the train had left. As I had made my adieux, I could not very well return to the house, and I had the choice of walking to Boston, a distance of some twenty miles - or spending the night out-of-doors. As it was warm, and a beautiful night, and as I was still not averse to be near my charmer, I went down on the beach and dug a hole in the warm sand, lay down and covered myself up, and with pleasant dreams rested comfortably until the chill of the morning, which came long before sunrise. I recollect clearly even now how cold I was when I awoke, and how I had to run around to get warm. I sat on the steps of various houses until sunrise, and, watching for activity in the girl's household, felt an increasing appetite for breakfast. I spied on her domicile until I saw her come out on the piazza, and then approaching, was received with much surprise. I explained what had occurred and joined the family at breakfast, with kind expressions from her parents to the effect that I was very foolish not to have returned and spent the night in a comfortable bed.

MOST of the summers of my youth were spent at the seashore. The earliest I remember were at Hyannisport, where I learned to swim when I was somewhere around the age of eight. In this sport my mother was the teacher rather than my father. Mother, who was born and brought up in Cohasset, had been quite a noted swimmer in her time, and on one occasion she had swum from Cohasset Narrows out around Minot's Light and back - a distance of about ten miles - quite a feat for those days.

There were several outstanding incidents in connection with that first summer spent at Hyannisport. Among my Chelsea friends there was Dana Evans, whose brother was in the United States Navy and was Commander of the schooner "Eager," a two masted, converted yacht (originally owned privately). Through some accident she had been sunk, and when raised she was fitted out for the United States Coast Survey. During that summer we were fortunate in having the schooner stationed at

Hyannis, where she lay back of the breakwater, from which point she made soundings and other surveys of that district.

My friendship with Dana gave me the privilege of frequently visiting the "Eager." To be ferried back and forth in the Captain's gig, with United States sailors to row us, gave us great distinction. Needless to say, Dana's brother was a great favorite with the ladies, and was often invited ashore to attend social functions.

On one of these occasions the gig was moored at a small pier, and the sailors were given shore-leave. Dana and I discovered the gig, which had a spritsail rolled up and laid along the thwarts. As there was a good breeze going, and we were eager to become sailors, this seemed an opportunity for us to learn. Unnoticed, we got the mast into position, and, as the wind was off shore, we had no difficulty in sailing away. When we realized that we were going off the land very fast, we decided to try to get back. This was quite another problem, as we knew little about tacking. Finally, realizing the impossibility of returning to our starting point, directly to windward, it became necessary to sail for another point which we could reach with the wind on our quarter. This point of sailing was quite as simple as running before the wind, but the direction led us away from our starting-place.

When we set out, we had no intention of being gone so long, and thought that we could get back without the boat being missed, furl up the sail, and leave everything for the sailors and the Captain when they returned. It became evident to us, after we had been away for hours, that the thing for us to do was to get ashore the best we could and disappear before we were caught. With the wind on the quarter, we were able to reach a large, stone pier at Hyannis. The breeze had come up, and we were going along at a rapid rate as we approached this wharf. Not knowing how to bring the boat into the wind, to make a proper landing, we struck this stone pier bow-on, smashing in several planks in the boat and snapping off the mast. This was a pretty predicament for us if caught! We tied the boat up to the wharf, on the windward side, and left her slowly filling with water. We made our escape. Needless to say, there was much enquiry. Dana's brother undoubtedly knew that we were the culprits, but under the circumstances he did not publicly announce it. After this experience we left government boats alone.

Another nautical experience occurred on a calm morning when I found a skiff anchored near the water's edge with some bait and fishing-lines which belonged to one of the older boys. I rowed the skiff out to the end of the breakwater, anchored, and started in to fish. It was not long before I hooked a fish and hauled it into the boat. Much to my astonishment, the belly began to swell out in a most astonishing manner. Never having seen a "puffer" (or, as some call it, a "Cape Cod minister," because it is so full of wind), I felt certain that I had caught a small sea-serpent. As the fish increased in size, my imagination led me to the decision that it would eventually rival the pictures of sea-serpents I had seen, and I became alarmed. I hated to let my prize go, as I felt that I had captured something that nobody else had ever seen, so, throwing it overboard, and making the line fast in the boat, I hauled up the anchor and started for the shore. As I landed on the beach, I rushed up to a lot of men who were working on a boat and told them that I had caught a sea-serpent. They saw how excited I was, and, running back with me, we pulled in the line, and there on the end was the poor Cape Cod minister!

My first sea-tragedy occurred either this summer, or a summer or two later, as my family went to Hyannisport for several seasons. Among my friends there was a boy, about fourteen years of age - a year or two older than I. He had a small catboat in which he used to take me out. One day we had gone off toward Point Gammon to catch sharks. There was a very light breeze when we started, but it stiffened up during the forenoon. As we started toward home because of the increased wind, I noticed objects bobbing about in the water about half a mile away. My friend was sailing the boat and we were going in that direction. I suggested that the objects in the water were people. He disagreed, calling my attention in a superior way to the fact that there was a fishing smack near these objects, which were probably buoys on fishing-nets. To confirm his statement, he called my attention to the fact that the smack had just put over a boat that was going in the direction I had indicated. I was insistent, however, that the objects were people, and he finally said that if I wanted to go over and see I would have to steer the boat.

I have always felt that he knew it was an accident just as I did, but had lost his nerve. At any rate, it did not take long to prove that the boat sent out from the smack was rescuing people from the water. When we got there, I, by that time knowing something about sailing, was able to put the boat alongside a woman who was hanging onto an oar. We hauled her aboard, and much to our surprise, discovered that there was a boy about twelve years old left hanging on the oar. He must have been covered up by the woman's floating skirt, as we had not previously noticed him. We also got him aboard. The boy was unconscious and the woman could not stand. We placed them both across the center-board box, face down, and water began to run out of their mouths. Nearby was another boy, trying to swim and crying for help, but before we could reach him, he disappeared. The boat from the fishing-smack had picked up the remainder and had started back for the ship.

We felt that it was best for us to place the woman and the boy on board the big boat with the others. The smack was laying quarter to the wind with her booms to leeward. On this account, we could not get up on the leeward side, and, as we went along on the windward side, some of the fishermen got our -passengers aboard. Naturally, our boom was lying across the smack's windward rail, so when it came down, hitting the rail, it broke off at about the middle. We were much excited. While we were on the smack everybody was crying "Is so and so here?" and the whole scene was most distressing. The man who owned the boat had taken a party of fourteen boys and women out for a sail. He apparently knew little about his boat, and it had capsized. When he learned that four of his party had been drowned, he was so depressed that he jumped overboard himself. Some of the sailors hooked onto him with fish-gaffs and pulled him back. They bound him with ropes and laid him on the deck.

The wind was increasing considerably, and we asked the smack's captain to tow us back to Hyannisport, where he was going with the survivors. This he refused to do in spite of the fact that we were only kids, and our boom was broken and our sail torn. He ordered us back into our small catboat and cast us off. We were really in a difficult position, but somehow we got our sail down and tied in two reefs after splinting the boom as best we could with a spare oar. We sailed back to Hyannisport and had quite a yarn to relate. As we did not return until late in the afternoon, our families were much worried, but when we told them of our adventure we were made to feel like real heroes. To my disgust, I learned afterwards that my companion became more of a hero than I thought he deserved, as he was given a medal for his ungracious part in the rescue.

The pier, where the fishing- and pleasure-boats tied up, was a place of great interest to me, and I had many friends among the fishermen. One of them had brought in a large sand-shark, which he had tied on to the deck. In his absence I was examining this fish, when a well-dressed summer-visitor, who had also been looking at the fish from the wharf, asked me if I wanted to sell "that swordfish." I knew sharks were of no value, and as he thought it was a swordfish, he amused me. I asked him how much he would give me for it, and he offered $25.00. I knew very well that my friend the fisherman would be glad to get $25.00 for a worthless shark, and immediately closed the transaction. The only stipulation I made was that the purchaser should take it away himself, but I offered to help him get it up on the wharf. He secured a large wheelbarrow, and together we loaded the shark into it after the man had given me the $25.00.

I could hardly wait until he got off the wharf with his purchase to make my escape. It took me but a short while to find my friend the fisherman, hand him the $25.00 and tell him the story. He thought it a great joke and was so sure it would not be long before the purchaser would find out what he had bought and come back, that he suggested our getting into the boat and taking a little sail. This we did and left the boat at the mooring when we returned. We later saw the purchaser on the dock, but took pains to avoid coming in contact with him.

MOVING ON

Going to college was an entirely new experience for me. I basically had not been away from home for any prolonged period of time during my life. Perhaps the longest was during my early years in high school when I went to Camp Waban on Lake Temagami in Ontario, Canada for two months. I happened to go with my close friend and Old Farm Rd gang member, Bob Mann, and another fellow student from Nobles. So that eased the anxiety there.

Heading off to mid-Florida to attend Rollins College was a completely new experience for me. First and foremost, I was going entirely on my own. I had not visited the college. I knew no one currently attending and nothing about the area where the college was located. In those days, I was a fairly large presence at 6' 3" and in good shape from playing football and rowing on the crew. All things in my favor. I did not really have a great deal of self-confidence, which was, I suppose, a self-imposed problem that was evident when I was made to go to dancing school. The whole process of which caused me to be self-centered or self-conscious. It somehow seemed that everyone was looking at me and if I made a mistake, everyone would see it. I was as nervous as could be asking any girl to dance, especially if I thought I liked her. Years later, it was obvious that everyone else was nervous and everyone else was focused on themselves rather than looking for someone to make fun of. Like so many things we experience, we internalize much of what we feel and think.

Some of that nervousness crept back as I headed off to Rollins College in Winter Park, FL. New place and absolutely no friends. Little did I know then that it would be one of the best and most beneficial lucky rolls of the dice that I would make. While Rollins was a long way from New England, I have to note that my father attended the college, but never graduated. It was after attending Rollins when I first read in my grandfather's book that Dr. Hamilton Holt, the first President of Rollins, was a patient of my grandfather and likely the reason my father attended the college.

Going away meant that I was no longer under the influence of my old gang of friends. Not that any of them were bad actors, but having to build new friends and relationships was very positive for me. It gave me a great deal of confidence in myself, which in retrospect was lacking in my high school years.

It also changed my attitude toward education. Two things happened. First, I got serious about learning and doing well in my studies. Next, without realizing it, Nobles had been able to pound a lot of knowledge into my head. At Rollins, from the get-go, I was an A student. That in itself was satisfying and exciting. At the end of my freshman year, I was asked by the Dean of Students if I would like to be a student councilor in the freshman dorm and help 10 freshmen students. I agreed and ultimately never left the freshman dorm for all four years. In my junior year, I was assigned the first black students to attend Rollins College. While not panicked, I was concerned about the general reaction, since this was a first for the college and to a great extent a first for me. My best description is that it was a non-event. I had not had any real interaction with people of color before that time and made an effort to treat them simply as freshmen students. There was no trouble at all in the dorm itself or on the campus that I was aware of. One of the students was a very outgoing and likable young man. The other was very quiet and shy keeping mostly to himself. He had a very hard time adjusting to college life and eventually left the college on his own.

At some point in my sophomore year, I was awarded a partial scholarship for my work as a student councilor and for academics.

Tuition was only about $3,000 per year back then or $27,500 in today's dollars, but getting something was a benefit to my father and certainly made me feel good about my education. At long last, my parents could be proud of what I was doing with my education. On top of that during my freshman year, I made the varsity crew. We had an excellent year winning most of our races. At the end of the season, we went to the Dad Vail regatta on the Schuylkill River near Philadelphia. This was supposed to be a small college event and a Rollins graduate said that if we won this regatta, he would pay for the crew to go to the Henley Regatta in England. We made it to the finals, but so did Northeastern University. They did not qualify as a small college but had been allowed to participate because they were new to crew. In the final race, we were bow to bow with NU and way ahead of the rest of the racers. Our bows would shift first position as we each took a stroke. Unfortunately, they were taking a stroke at the right time and beat us by 6 inches.

While at Rollins, I kept up with my fishing and hunting. Fishing was easy as the college is surrounded by lakes that had extensive populations of largemouth bass and a good supply of baitfish to keep them happy and well fed. I found several other friends who liked to fish, and we got our share of action. I did not often travel back to New England during school year vacations but would head to the Florida Keys or Everglades to fish for tarpon and snook, something I had done with my father and continued to do.

Hunting was another story. There were a number of hunting opportunities, but none of them right near the college. One thing that would be completely different than today was that we kept our guns right in our dorm room. I had a shotgun, a rifle and a handgun. I was not the only one and no one really got concerned about that. It was a different time for sure. I do know that the resident advisor and in my junior and senior years, I was the assistant resident advisor, asked me to leave the rifle and handgun ammo in his apartment, but when I was going hunting it would be easily available.

We hunted mostly ducks, snipe and doves. We tried our luck at hogs but were unsuccessful. The duck and snipe hunting took place on Lake Kissimmee south of Orlando. On my first trip with some other students who lived locally, we motored the boat into the water hyacinth that appeared to be along the shoreline so we could jump out and wade to shore. The next thing I know, the other guys start jumping over the side holding their guns and ammo over their heads. No one wore any waders. The water came up to their chests as they pushed through the thick plants. I was by far the last to jump over. As I have said, the idea of snakes doesn't really bother me, unless we are talking about poisonous snakes and ones you cannot see. The second they saw my hesitancy, they were all over me about watching out and laughingly saying, "don't get bit!" I didn't. We hunted there quite a lot, but I only saw one water moccasin and that was when I was on solid ground.

Opening day of duck hunting at Lake Kissimmee while at Rollins.

There were also alligators around in just about all the lakes there, but there were nowhere near as many as today. I don't know it for a fact, but my guess was that they had been hunted for a while around the time I attended college. When that stopped, they began to repopulate the local lakes. Just a guess. But there was a lot of water activity at the college with swimming and water skiing. I do not remember any bad interaction with an alligator. Also, back then, the whole area now developed into Disney World Orlando was just orange groves. Disney did not exist there at all. Today, Disney has completely transformed the whole area.

Some of my classmates from Nobles who went to Harvard would come south for a visit. I was usually able to find a place for them to stay. They would be simply missing classes to take the trip. Mostly, they wanted to play golf. They'd say, "let's play golf today." And in most instances I would have to reply, "I can't." They always wanted to know why? The reason was that Rollins had a no-cut class policy. If you weren't in class you better have a good reason and golf was not one that was accepted. Most of my northern friends could not understand that policy as Harvard had predominantly lecture courses where the only obligation was to show up for exams.

During college years, I had a variety of summer jobs mostly based near the Wareham area. One year I tried working at Cape Cod Cultured Clam Corp. in Orleans, MA, but that entailed an hour plus drive each way, so I did not last the entire summer. Too much travel time. Then I worked doing brush clearing with a friend and made some decent money and still had time to do a little fishing. This was manual labor and occasionally required lifting that should have been done by some sort of machine. We didn't have anything like the required machinery, so our backs had to suffice. I injured my back and had to stop that job. Physical therapy just did not exist in those days, and I did all sorts of things that were suggested. While my back calmed down by the end of summer, I had problems with it back at college and trying to continue rowing on the varsity crew. I was dropped to the JV boat and somewhere in the season simply stopped rowing.

One summer, my father had purchased a franchise for a Howdy Beefburger fast food restaurant. It was the precursor to McDonalds. He asked if I wanted to work there for a summer and I said sure. Part of the job would be helping to get the place set up and ready to open as well as working there after. So, my father and I had to do some training at a Howdy Beefburger in Dedham on Route 1. We took a stint at every different job. We worked the fryolator, making french fries. We flipped burgers on the grill. We wrapped the burgers for sale. We worked the cash register and worked the customer windows. I distinctly remember one day some friends of my father came up to the window. They saw both of us working there and kept their heads down while ordering and pretending not to see us. I'm sure they thought that the Cunningham's had fallen on hard times. It was interesting to watch and slightly amusing. My father's restaurant was in Brockton, MA and originally was supposed to be built next to a Dunkin Donuts. DD's next to the burger joints never happened and unfortunately Howdy Beefburger never turned into McDonalds.

The manager who ran the restaurant was fair to work for, but very strict about the rules he set. The day all the staff started to work, he gathered everyone and laid down the rules. His enforcement was like baseball, and he was the umpire. If you messed up he simply called a strike. 3 strikes and you were out. One morning, I had not paid attention to the clock and arrived 5 minutes late. He just looked up and said, "Strike one." Nothing else. I never got another strike and somewhere in the mid-summer took on the assistant manager job. Looking back, it was a good education working with new and different people and just a little bit out of my comfort zone.

MORE NEW EXPERIENCES

y senior year, I started with a Master's program at the Crummer School of Business, which was part of Rollins and only in the program's second year. I was doing fine, but I did not really like the program. The way it was designed, and its general thrust felt that it was not going to be useful for me. It had a far stronger interest in economics, and I was more interested in business finance. So, I thought long and hard and decided that I would just graduate with my class and move on with my life. I did that fully realizing that the US was involved in the Vietnam War and since there was a draft, which required one to enlist in the military, I would have to serve in some capacity. After, I left Florida and returned to Dover, I began the search for an officer's candidate school that would let me in. I did not want to be drafted into the Army and felt that Army officer's candidate school was my last choice. So, on to the Navy. Not a chance. They were not taking any more candidates. Next was the Coast Guard. I filled out all the paperwork and again I was turned down for lack of space. This was getting serious as I had a set period of time to get something done before I received my draft notice. On to the US Marines. They said yes, and I nervously raised my hand and was sworn in. Luckily, it was June and the class I signed up for did not start until January.

So, now I had to find something to make a little money while I waited for the class to start and while I anticipated my getting a major whoop-ass from a drill sergeant with a wicked bad attitude. It just so happened that my good friend from Old Farm Rd, Spider

Andresen, was working on pulling together a crew for a swordfish harpoon boat which would be running out of New Bedford. So, I signed on for the rest of the summer.

Heading out of New Bedford on a trip aboard the Jaguar.

The vessel, called the *Jaguar*, belonged to an eye doctor from Annisquam, MA, Fred Breed, later to be nicknamed Fearless Freddie. He got that name on the first day we were heading out to sea. He was out on the pulpit securing the harpoon and we crashed into a rather large wave. Freddie, the pulpit, and the bow disappeared in the water only to reemerge with him grasping both sides of the stand railing where only the center section of the harpoon remained. He looked back at us and extended his arm and index finger out to sea. Fearless Freddie was born.

Some of the crew of the *Jaguar*.
L to R. The author, Chico Weber, Peter Buckley, and Russell Cleary.

Jaguar was a Grand Banks schooner of 86 feet. The top of the mainmast was around 100 feet and had a place for a lookout. Most of the time our fish spotter/lookout was Russell Cleary. To get to the top he would climb the ratlins, essentially a ladder made between two cable wire stays. But to get down, he would slide down the aft stay with his bare hands, usually headfirst. Never had a problem. The foremast was close to length of the boat and had controls to steer and adjust the speed. The harpoon stand extended out from the bow about 20 feet. The main salon of the schooner had been taken out and converted to an insulated fish hold which took ice and then fish as we caught them after they had been headed and gutted. Getting the fish ready for the ice hold usually took until dark or after. Then we'd chow down and hit the bunks. Getting up and ready to go by sunrise.

Swordfish on deck and sword about to be removed to prevent damage or injury.

Peter Buckley cleaning swordfish. A messy process at best.

Fred not only was the captain and harpooner. He was also the cook. Most of his cooking was directly on top of the cast iron kerosine stove. Fried eggs, on the stove top. Seared steaks on the stove top. The only problem was that doing this caused Fred to get seasick. So, if it was at all rough, he'd be cooking away, then stick his head out the companionway and throw up. That made for interesting and sometime humorous talk about what was for dinner!

Fearless Freddie as the harpooner was darn good. Sometimes our spotter pilot, Art Singerless, would talk the boat onto a fish that he could see from up in the air, but we could not. Many times, Fred was able to the put the harpoon in the right spot while never having seen the fish. I was the dory man and had to go over the side in a dory to haul the fish back after the harpoon was struck. Out from the harpoon head came a line to an inner tube about 30 feet back and then about 50 yds of line and a tall bouy. The partially inflated inner tube kept the fish from diving straight to the bottom as the inner tube was always trying to pull it back to the surface. The dory had a steel plate in the bottom to protect against a swordfish trying to puncture the bottom of the dory. Only once did I have a swordfish charge me in the dory. I knew it was going to be a problem fish. Right after being struck with the harpoon, it streaked across the surface then turned and attacked the inner tube with its sword. The fish tried to ram the dory from the side a number of times, but just thumped its back and dorsal fin on the bottom. Exciting, none-the-less.

One of the other swordfish boats had a dory man who did not have any kind of steel plate or protection on the bottom of the dory. He was sitting on the bottom pulling a swordfish and the fish came straight up from under the dory. The sword penetrated through the bottom and ran up his spine. They found him sitting bolt upright and dead.

Spider ran the controls at the top of the foremast and could hear the pilot telling him and Fred where the fish was. Most of the time they could see the quarry. And once he had the fish in his sight, Fred had Spider turn off the speaker. Whenever possible I would stand up near the harpoon stand to get a good idea where the fish was hit. If it was well struck, then I knew it could be pulled in forcefully. If Fred didn't like the hit, then it was a two finger pull. Some days, I would go over the side into the dory in the morning and never get back on the big boat until sunset. That meant that I might have two or three fish with their tails tied up to the dory's gunwale at any one time. I hoped that they would stay alive enough to keep their swords moving back and forth. This kept the sharks away. Sometimes, I had to jab a hungry shark with a lance that I kept in the dory, but over the summer, I never lost a bite to a shark.

Our spotter pilot, Art Singerless buzzing the *Jaguar*.

Our spotter pilot, Art Singerless, who went on the become an Eastern Airlines pilot, liked to play pranks on us first thing in the morning when he flew out from Martha's Vineyard. He would call on the radio and ask where we were, saying that he couldn't find us. The first time we wondered why he couldn't see us, then he came screaming out of the morning sunrise where we had been unable to see him. A gotcha. After that we knew that we had to be straining our eyes to look into the sun. One time when the sun was just coming over the horizon he was flying so close to the water that he misjudged when to pull up to go over the boat. He had to roll the plane on its side and put the wing between the two masts. No problem. On another occasion, he suddenly radioed us that he had to head to shore. The cap on the engine oil fill was right in front of the windshield. The cap came off and wind pulling up and over the windshield was sucking all the engine oil out. He was overheating and afraid that he'd have to ditch in the ocean. As he headed to shore another spotter pilot asked him if he had any spare oil. He said that he did. The response was, "well put it in and plug the oil fill." Art replied, "it's gonna be hard trying to fly the plane sitting out on the strut, then putting the oil in and getting it plugged." The other pilot replied that he better start learning and he did. Art made it back to the airport, filled up the oil reservoir, got a new fill cap, and headed back out for the rest of the day.

Our best day that summer was 19 fish. It was a day that everyone was finding a lot of fish, so Fred decided that we would head in to New Bedford to get ahead of the other boats and make sure that the market was not flooded with fish. It was a good decision as the market had been tight and we got the best price of the summer at 40 cents a pound for headed and gutted fish. The boats that stayed out an extra day did not get that price. Today swordfish generally sells for $15 per pound.

A big swordfish on the *Jaguar* deck

We did not make a lot of money, but being out offshore for a week a trip was a real experience. At that time, there was no 200 Mile Limit and foreign vessels could come right in as close as 3 miles from shore. We fished around the Southeast Corner, so named as it was the southern end of Georges Bank. It was a very productive fishing ground and the Russian factory trawlers were there in numbers. At night, it looked like a small city out on the horizon. They generally did not come close to where we would heave to for the night, which was right next to a marker called The Corner Bouy as it marked the southern corner of the bank. We did not set an anchor, but raised a small sail and lashed the helm hard over. Then we sailed in slow circles all night and would be in the same general area in the morning.

One day while fishing, we pulled alongside of one of the factory ships. A bunch of the Russian sailors looked down at us from the high sides. We decided to toss them a few beers. What we tossed were cans and they had never seen them before. We took one held it up and pulled the tab to open. When they did it, the beer sprayed out as the cans had been tossed up and landed on the deck. We shook one up and did the same thing. We all laughed, and they drank what we tossed up to them after that. The Russian factory trawlers and processors took an incredible amount of fish from what should have been our sovereign territory. I suspect they also did whatever surveillance they could. Luckily, in 1976 the US got all foreign fishing vessels out of our waters with the passage of the 200 Mile Limit bill known as the Magnuson–Stevens Fishery Conservation and Management Act. Legislation that I would learn a lot about later in life.

OUTWARD BOUND

In early September, I was out in the dory pulling in a fish. A spotter pilot from one of the other boats came overhead, idled back his engine, and yelled out the window, "Cunningham, call the Coast Guard!" What was wrong I wondered? When I got back to the boat, I got on the ship to shore radio and talked to Woods Hole Coast Guard. They told me that there was an opening in two weeks for Coast Guard officers candidate school (OCS) and did I want it? Yes, was the emphatic answer. Now I had to get to shore and luckily did not have to pull a mutiny to get Freddie to head into New Bedford. That ended my days at sea chasing swordfish, which likely made my mother very happy. On my days off, I would drive to Dover with a plastic bag of clothes that were stinky ripe with fish guts smell. Cleaning swordfish was not for the faint of heart and many nights after starting fishing at sunrise, we'd be cleaning and icing until after dark and be covered in fish blood and slime. When my mother would open the bag to get the clothes in the washing machine, she would almost pass out. After a couple of times, I had to do my own laundry.

My next chore was to get out of the Marines and sworn into the Coast Guard, and do it quickly. Luckily, my father had been on Senator Ed Brooke's finance team during his election campaign. I asked if he would call the Senator and request help with this issue. In a matter of days, I had been transferred and sworn in. I flew to Washington, DC and spent a couple of nights with my old Nobles roommate, Harry Stimpson, and he was kind enough to drive me to Yorktown, VA where I would spend the next few months. After getting a very short buzz cut and being issued basic uniform gear, every day, except Sunday, was pretty much the same. Get up in the dark and do a group run for 30 to 45 minutes. Then calisthenics. Get cleaned up and tidy your room. March off to breakfast. Then classes until lunch followed by some activity such as marching drill, rescue practice or pistol training.

On the first day of pistol training, we shot with .22 caliber weapons. They were fairly decent shooting pistols. I scored fairly well and thought that I'd be able to get my marksman ribbon to add to my uniform. We used those several times and then changed to .45 caliber weapons to qualify. When I picked up my weapon, it rattled like a marble in an empty coffee can. It had been shot so much that every moving part was completely worn out. The next problem was that the trigger would activate when my finger even got close. This made trying to hit a target a big problem. On my practice round, I put at least one bullet in the overhead in front of the firing bench. I could barely get a bullet in the target. When it came time for the qualifying round, I simply shot at targets on either side hoping to help my classmates get a ribbon, as I knew it was not possible for me to get one. After the round, we had to stand next to our targets and the gunnery officer would come up and look at it. He looked at mine and said, "Cunningham, if they send you to Vietnam, remember to save two bullets for yourself." I did my best not to laugh.

I can honestly say that going through this military process was a positive for me. Like heading off to college, it was going to a whole new place where I had to answer to others and had to make new friends. What I soon found was that the friends I made during this school were temporary. We supported each other during the process, but we immediately went in different directions and had little chance to meet up again.

One fun event that our platoon took part in was a Veterans Day parade at the famous Yorktown Battleground where the American revolution essentially ended. It was an inter-military marching event where each platoon would be judged for their marching and arms presentation. Out of several at Coast Guard OCS, our platoon was chosen. We had practiced and practiced, but likely so had the others. As we approached the review stand on the Battleground, our steps sounded like one man marching. During the arms presentation, the bolt opening of the 40 weapons sounded as one and so did the closing with a single loud clack. All of us knew that we had nailed it. We took first place against all the other military branches. The Commandant of the school was very happy and as I remember we got one Saturday off from barracks inspection, which was another weekly event that most dreaded. You had to have perfectly made your bed, organized your uniforms which you would have washed and ironed, spit and polished your dress shoes, and polish all your brass. The routine was that the officer of the day went through everything with white gloves that had better be just as white after the inspection. Failure at inspection usually meant that you'd have the privilege of polishing some large piece of brass, likely a cannon, around the parade grounds. I did my share of polishing as everyone did. For the first half of the school, it did not matter how much you worked on making your room and gear perfect, something would be found unsatisfactory. That lightened up in the second half of the 17-week program.

One other training skill that we had to learn was in what was called the Combat Information Center. This mimicked what would be found on a military ship. It essentially was the control center for navigating the ship and maneuvering it in and around other ships. Each of us had a turn at being the officer-in-charge. You would see a ship off in the distance on the radar and quick calculations would say that you were on a collision course, so you would give the helmsman orders to alter the course to a new heading that you determined to avoid collision. As soon as that happened, one of the unseen instructors would alter the other ship's course so you were back on collision courses. You'd alter again and so would the other ship. All the while the instructor watching you was incessantly asking you what are you going to do in a louder and louder voice. Eventually, collision is imminent, and he is practically shouting "What are you going to do." I finally, said, "Sir, I am calling the Captain and telling him to put on his swimming trunks." It was not deemed to be as amusing as I thought it was, but I didn't have to do any extracurricular brass polishing.

I entered OCS at 246 pounds and 17 weeks later, I graduated at 173 pounds. I had to buy all new clothes, but most of those were uniforms that I needed to buy anyway. The whole experience was beneficial. I had to interact with a lot of people from varied backgrounds. We leaned on each other and learned how to support each other. While I have regretted not applying for flight school and learning to fly helicopters, I do not know how different my life would have been. If I had gone into the Marines and had been sent to Vietnam, it would certainly have been different. I had several friends who went there and did not return alive. Others were there and came home as very different people. None of those returning received the wholehearted welcome that they deserved. It was a very strange time.

I was stationed back in Boston and during that time there were daily anti-Vietnam War demonstrations outside the J F Kennedy Building, where Coast Guard District 1 headquarters were. We were told not to wear uniforms to work, so we could easily get through the demonstrators. Most of my duties had to do with supporting the educational efforts and boat inspection services of the Coast Guard Auxiliary. The members of the Auxiliary were a wonderful group of folks who performed a great service to the boating public. A secondary duty was being the Admiral's aide. This meant that I had gold braid around my left shoulder and accompanied the Admiral to many events and helped him when needed or requested. It gave me some "power" as I could say to any senior ranking officer that "the Admiral would like….!" and it would get done. I was the aide to Admiral William Ellis. He was a great person and very near the end of a 36-year career in service. On my first time as aide, I was as nervous as can be. Admirals were like gods, but I soon learned that they put their pants on one leg at a time, just like the rest of us. At one event, my fiancee, North

Lyman and I had to climb down a ship ladder into a cabin with the admiral and other officers. The Admiral went over and moved the men away so they could not look up North's skirt. He was a wonderful and kind man.

Two things stick out in my mind with this duty. The first was a harbor cruise aboard a 210 foot cutter, I believe called the Vigilant, for members of the Coast Guard Auxiliary. While I worked with the folks in the Auxiliary, I was also the Admiral's aide on this trip. We had been outside the harbor and were on our way back in. Coming down the harbor was the aircraft carrier Wasp. She was leaving Boston for a change of station. It is a long-standing tradition of ships to render honors to another ship that has a superior ranking officer on board. Well, the officer of the deck on the Coast Guard cutter was scanning the flags on the Wasp with binoculars. He turned to the Admiral and said, "Sir, they have no flag rank (Admiral) on board!" The Admiral was beaming and said, "Don't render honors until they do." Then the officer of the deck said, "Admiral, they have seen your flag and they are running around the bridge." The ships were moving slowly, but within minutes a platoon of Marines was on the foredeck of the Wasp in full dress uniforms. As we passed, the massive aircraft carrier, dipped its flags to honor the Admiral and the much smaller cutter responded as all onboard saluted the other ship. The Admiral grinning from ear-to-ear loudly remarked, "We'll have some fun with this at the monthly area commanders meeting."

The second event that remains vivid in my memory was the Simas Kudirka affair. When this took place Admiral Ellis was on sick leave after having some serious surgery. Captain Fletcher Brown was the acting District Commander. Simas, a Lithuanian, was the radioman on a Soviet fishing boat that carried some Soviet negotiators for fisheries. The ship was tied alongside of the Vigilant south of Martha's Vineyard. Kudirka tossed a message onto the Vigilant that he intended to defect. Since these meeting had been set up by the State Department and since all secure communications had to go through Washington and the State Department in those days, there were many delays in information getting back and forth. Some of the delays were at least an hour. It was a far cry from instant communications available today. The District Commander's office was not a place to be that afternoon. Captain Brown had no idea of what to do either before or after Simas jumped onto the Cutter. He was panicked to say the least. The Captain of the Vigilant was reluctant to return Simas. Captain Brown had called Admiral Ellis a number of times asking for advice. Admiral Ellis did not want to comment as he had not seen any of the messaging. Finally, Captain Brown practically begged him for advice. The Admiral reluctantly said that it was standard protocol to return all defectors during negotiations. Captain Brown then ordered Simas returned. The Captain of the Vigilant did not directly obey the order and after forcefully pulling away from the fishing ship allowed the Russian sailors to come onto the Vigilant, which was standing by alongside the Soviet fishing vessel. Then he allowed the Russian sailors to chase Simas down. After being caught, he was hog tied and throw down off the deck into the small boat that took them all back to the Soviet vessel. Since, this was during the height of the Cold War with Russia, President Nixon had to get involved and said that whoever allowed this to happen would be dealt with harshly. Both Captain Brown and Admiral Ellis were court martialed. Captain Brown said that he had been ordered by Admiral Ellis to return the defector. Not true, but an unfortunate case of being in the wrong place at the wrong time for the Admiral. Just as he was about to retire, the Admiral was thrown out of the Coast Guard after 36 years. Captain Brown was as well. The Captain of the Vigilant, who caused damage to the cutter and Russian ship and allowed the Russian sailors to run at will on a US military ship received only a letter of reprimand. Simas was sent to Siberia for some period of time and then was able to immigrate to the US, where he eventually became a citizen.

I was and remain proud of my military service and still feel that it would be beneficial for many. You definitely see things differently after having the experience and it gives a real sense of respect for all those who serve and protect our country as a way of life. It was great to be a part of our country's military.

IV

FORECASTING THE FUTURE

JOHN H CUNNINGHAM

*T*HE SECOND phase of my life that I consider worth recording is the tracing of those influences which, during childhood and boyhood days, drove me inevitably toward the profession which has been my life work. The question of selecting a vocation is one that enters vitally into every life, and the influences that affected me will recall, in the minds of the readers of these pages, incidents which pointed then towards or away from the natural expression of their own separate personalities.

The essentials of potential success in a boy, as I see them, are:

1. *Health.* (Even this only in the degree to make possible the standard striven for.)
2. *Energy.* (This may be only an expression of health, and often misdirected.)
3. *An Ideal.* (Usually an older person who becomes the boy's hero.)

4. *Confidence.* (This may be born of some trivial accomplishment, which supplies the incentive for concentration.)

Making a personal application of these essentials, I am sure that those who have read the preceding pages will cheerfully give me credit for possessing the first two. I have no doubt that a continuing major problem in the minds of my parents was how my tireless energy could be controlled and directed into constructive channels. While I have always believed that my Ideal was of my own selection, and that Confidence came to me from outside the family, it is at least probable that my parents are entitled to far more credit than I have ever given them. Such is the universal lack of understanding in children - unappreciated by them until they themselves become parents! Be that as it may. There is no doubt in my own mind that my early interest in medicine and surgery was the direct result of the stories I heard in the family circle of my uncle, Dr. William Cunningham, who resisted all attempts to divert him from the calling he selected - at great personal sacrifice; I am convinced that this early interest was inflamed into a definite purpose by the discovery of Uncle Will's grisly relics in Grandmother's house; I feel certain that the definite purpose was finally set for me by the unexpected understanding of a deeply revered teacher, who recognized something besides mischief in a pupil's interest in the dissecting of cats.

A PLACE that I enjoyed visiting as a boy was the now famous shipyard of Donald MacKay, which was located in East Boston. At that time, we had no idea that MacKay, who was just completing the group of famous clipper-ships of that period, would ever become so famous in the history of the American Merchant Marine. Another shipyard was that owned by D. D. Kelly, also in East Boston. While Kelly never became as noted as Donald MacKay, he nevertheless built many of

Massachusetts' greatest clippers. I little realized in those days that here, in Kelly's shipyard, my future career was being definitely influenced.

The vessel which Kelly happened to be completing at that time was christened "The Great Surgeon." Dr. William K. Thorndike, the man for whom the ship was named, was one of the pioneer surgeons of Massachusetts, a member of the first staff of the Boston City Hospital, and one of that group of famous men which included Dr. Henry Bigelow and Dr. David Cheever. Dr. Thorndike, who lived in East Boston, had performed an operation upon Kelly's son, and there is no question that through his skill he had saved the boy's life. Old Kelly was so grateful that he told the owners of the boat that he would not finish it unless he had the privilege of naming it. He was granted this privilege, and he called the ship "The Great Surgeon."

Kelly sent to Germany, which was then a very unusual thing to do, and had a bust of Doctor Thorndike made as a figurehead to go under the bowsprit. This ship had a great career, went all over the world, and I have always felt that no member of the medical profession ever had a greater honor paid to him.

This whole affair produced a deep impression upon me. Here was a profession in which a man could achieve the distinction of having a ship named in his honor! My imagination could conceive of no greater personal satisfaction, and from that moment the frequent references I heard made to my Uncle Will in the family discussions assumed a new and peculiar significance.

Uncle Will had insisted upon studying medicine when he had the option of going into the boiler- and pipe-works with his father and two brothers. The family enterprise, one of the oldest in Boston, held no interest for him. Sufficient difficulties were put in his way by his father to make sure that this determination was basic, but when the boy met and overcame these, the family yielded. Uncle Will went through the Harvard Medical School, and became an interne of the Boston City Hospital, graduating in 1880. He afterwards became City Physician in Charlestown and was later connected with the anatomical department of the Harvard Medical School. I might add, in this connection, that Dr. D. J. Cunningham, a graduate of the University of Edinburgh, Professor of Anatomy and Surgery in the University of Dublin, one of the greatest anatomists of his time, and the author of Cunningham's "Anatomy," which is used all over the world and which I studied in the Medical School, was William Cunningham's father's brother.

What gave Uncle Will the desire to pursue the same course as his uncle I never knew, but I remember his uniform kindness to me as a small boy, and his pleasure in finding me interested to look over his anatomy books with him. He was a great student of anatomy, and even had in his house bodies which he dissected. The story goes that his father used to object to this, so Uncle Will had to hide his "stiffs" in his bedroom. Then, after the old gentleman retired, he would get up and continue his laboratory work. As far as I know, he was never caught. Later, somewhere around the late '80s, he went to England. He spent some time in the hospitals of London and Edinburgh and became associated with his uncle in the anatomical department of the University of Dublin.

About that time the Plague of the Peninsula broke out, and as Uncle Will was one of the young men versed in the use of the microscope, which had only recently come into vogue, he went on the English expedition to Spain and Portugal, and did excellent work This was brought to my attention by Dr. Harold Ernst, Professor of Bacteriology at Harvard, with whom I did some special work on fish fungi while a student. Professor Ernst also drew my attention to the fact that Uncle Will was the first American ever to become a fellow of Royal College of Surgeons.

Later, when the War of the Sudan had reached the crisis in which the reserves had to be called out from England, Uncle Will went as surgeon to the regiment known as the "Queen's Own," of Edinburgh, the Colonel of which was another uncle - a brother of his father's. Uncle Will was at the fall of Alexandria, and later received the Victoria Cross for bravery on the field.

I recollect seeing an autograph letter from Queen Victoria, expressing her appreciation. Following the War of the Sudan, he returned to London and became surgeon and demonstrator of anatomy at King's College Hospital. While still in this capacity, he was honored by being introduced at Court; later he married Lady X., one of Queen Victoria's Ladies-in-waiting. They lived in Leamington Spa, and my sister, Sarah, has a large oil-painting of the place, given to her when she was visiting them somewhere around 1905.

Uncle Will and his wife visited Grandmother in Charlestown on a few occasions, but Lady X. made herself thoroughly unpopular by her caustic comparisons of American customs and "the way we do it in England." Their stays in this country were brief. Uncle Will had become a great swell. He never made a cent in his life, living on the estate which his father had left him. He died some time in his fifties of pneumonia. His widow, who, I believe, must have had some fortune of her own, erected a marble monument in the cemetery in Leamington Spa, with a clock at the top, and an endowment fund to maintain a man to care for the monument. Likewise, there was established, I don't know by whose money but by the direction of his widow, the Cunningham Ambulance Service at King's Hospital in London. In 1913, the only time I ever visited London, the ambulance service was still in operation.

ALL these activities of Uncle Will's had a definite effect on my interest in medicine, and I always considered him a model to be copied. He became a hero in my mind in spite of the fact that he was the object of much criticism in the family. My boyish estimate was not in accord with the point of view that to be a consumer and not a producer necessarily made a man a parasite. I believed that anybody who had done so much in the field of medicine, and who had been made a F.R.C.S., and had received the Victoria Cross, had really accomplished much, in spite of the fact that he had never attempted to make money.

Once, when I was prowling about in my grandmother's attic, I found, in a coffin-like box, a partially dissected body, which Uncle Will had evidently been working on at home. He had left it tucked away in the attic when he went off to Europe. Most of the muscles of the body were present and as hard as wood. I was at once filled with a desire to clean the muscles off and then mount the skeleton.

On the following Saturday, when there was no school, my friend Billy Robinson went with me to Grandmother's house in Charlestown. In the seclusion of the attic we dressed the body with trousers and shoes, together with a shirt and an outer wrap, which was a heavy dressing-gown - all found among the many things stored away in the garret. I put a hat on the old fellow and a muffler around his ghastly face. We each took the skeleton by one arm, and, by great good luck, got out of the house unobserved. Then we went down to the end of Chestnut Street, where we waited for the horse-car. This was wintertime. With care we helped our invalid into the car, in which there were several people but still there was plenty of room to sit down. Some of the passengers were quite touched by the scene, and enquired if the poor old gentleman, who must be very feeble, would not like to have a seat. We informed them that he much preferred to stand up. The real facts were that the skeleton was so stiff that there was no way of bending the joints. We paid his fare and arrived at my home in Chelsea without being discovered. Then we stood the skeleton up in the linen closet, carefully concealed.

The next morning being Sunday, we started on our job of cleaning off the muscles by cutting some of them with a saw, so that we could double the skeleton up in the set vat in the laundry. The vat was too shallow to permit the cover to go down, and it rested on the head, leaving the top up about a foot. After the water got boiling, a highly flavored steam filled the laundry and escaped up the clothes-chute, permeating the rooms with which it was connected. We had a Catholic servant who, perceiving the odor in the chambers, came to the laundry to find out the cause, it being evident that the fumes were coming up from that locality. We heard her coming, ran out of the laundry, and hid in the coal-bin, which was so located that we could look directly into the laundry.

The maid, upon entering, saw the vat-cover bobbing up and down with the skull surrounded by steam. She let out a yell, fell on her knees, began to cross herself, and then rolled over in a dead faint. We rushed in and dragged her out, shut the door and locked it, and proceeded as fast as possible to put out the fire beneath the vat. Soon Father appeared, and insisted upon the door being opened, which command could not be resisted. The skeleton was finally cleaned and mounted, and remained in my possession for many years. At present it is at the Charlesgate Hospital in Cambridge, where it is still used in the nurses' class.

Another relic I found among Uncle Will's effects was a human ear, carefully tucked away in a small box. This trophy might have come from some important person, as it was not only carefully packed but had a short description written on the box, the significance of which I have forgotten. This ear, in appearance, resembled a dried apricot. It became one of my prized possessions, and I used to carry it about with me occasionally to horrify friends.

In my class at the Carter School was a young lady, Amy Mayo, in whom I was much interested. Occasionally, I would pass candy over to her during class, which she would eat at opportune moments. One day, when I happened to have the ear in my pocket and no candy, I noticed a glance of inquiry which I interpreted as a request for the usual sweet. I took the ear out of the box and slipped it over to her. To my horror, she accepted it in good faith, and was slipping it into her mouth. I tried frantically to attract her attention, but failed. Then I called to her, "Don't eat that. It's a human ear! "

This caused her to scream, and she threw the ear on the floor. Naturally, the teacher became interested, as well as the rest of the class. I was asked to stand up and give an explanation of what it all meant. The teacher asked where the ear was, and I pointed to the floor. In the meantime, Amy had become hysterical, as any sensitive girl should. The teacher came down the aisle and started to pick the ear up, but when she saw that it really was a human fragment, she drew back and would not touch it. I was ordered to retrieve it and put it on her desk. After I had obeyed, she returned to her desk, took one look at the grisly object, and then ordered me to take it away. While I was severely punished, nevertheless I recovered the ear, and it has always remained a prized possession.

IN the Fall of 1892, I was sent to Hopkinson's School, on Chestnut Street in Boston, to prepare for Harvard. The house then used as the school was one of the oldest on Beacon Hill, and was formerly the home of Edwin Booth, the actor. It was about a ten-minute walk from the school to the Massachusetts General Hospital, and, as school was dismissed at eleven o'clock on Saturday mornings, and as that was the public operating-day in the amphitheater at that hospital, I decided that I would like to go there and watch the operating.

On my first visit I was refused admittance because of my youth. Undaunted by this rebuff, I conceived the idea of going to the Out-patient Department, where, under pretense of some ailment, I gained admission. This Department was then in the old Bigelow Amphitheatre Building. At an opportune moment, it was simple to slip out of the waiting-room, where so many were sitting on long settees, and find my way into the amphitheater.

This became a regular Saturday morning performance all through that school year. As a result, I had the privilege of observing some of the very early abdominal surgery by such pioneers as J. Collins Warren, Arthur Cabot, Dr. John Homans, Dr. Henry Beach, Dr. C. B. Porter, and many of the younger men - Dr. Maurice Richardson and others who later became famous. The room was named in honor of Doctor Bigelow, and on one of the posts, beside the seats, was the apparatus known as the Lister Spray. I never saw this in use, as antiseptic surgery was just being supplanted by aseptic surgery. Nevertheless, the surgeons still wore butchers' frocks. There were no gloves, and the sponges used were sea-sponges which were kept in antiseptic solutions after being boiled and kept in order by old Jim Mains.

This early surgery, as I remember, included amputations, particularly legs and arms; removal of jaws and tongues for cancer; and breast-operations. Abdominal surgery was very seldom practiced at that time. There were occasional appendix-operations, this condition never being recognized until abscess-formation. The operation consisted largely of emptying the abscess, and not at all the appendix-operation which is now so common. In fact, the disease appendicitis was not recognized as such until Dr. Reginald Fitz described it in a monograph on that subject (1886).

The ligatures used were largely silk, but Dr. Henry Marcy, of Cambridge, was at that time popularizing kangaroo-tendon and catgut. The catgut, as I recollect it, seemed to be the suture and ligature most appreciated, especially by Drs. C. B. Porter and Maurice Richardson.

After hearing a long discourse by Doctor Porter about catgut-suture and having seen it used in an operation for ovarian-cyst which he removed, and having seen Doctor Richardson use a similar suture in removing an appendix and sewing up the abdomen, I had a great desire to try to use it myself.

V

OBSERVED IN THE HOSPITAL CLINIC

JOHN H CUNNINGHAM

*T*HERE is probably no place that offers a better opportunity to study human nature than a hospital clinic. Here the Doctor is brought into intimate contact with patients of every nationality and representing every walk in life. Here one finds displayed every human attribute from deepest suspicion and antagonism to fullest confidence and gratitude. The following anecdotes, still retained in my recollection of that period in my life, will give an idea of how work in a hospital clinic forces the Doctor to run the gamut of human emotions.

MRS. SULLIVAN was the mother of eight children. In the Fall of 1908, an epidemic of diphtheria of the most malignant character swept through the Boston district in which she lived. In response to her appeal for aid at the hospital, the Doctor found four of her children acutely ill with the disease. They were bundled into the ambulance and carried to the hospital. As is so commonly the case in diphtheria, these children had developed membranes in the throat of such size and obstructing nature as to require opening the windpipe. Even this was hopeless - each child in turn died.

Mrs. Sullivan was brokenhearted. A week after the death of the fourth child, she appeared at the hospital carrying her oldest remaining boy, now also afflicted with the disease. She looked at the Doctor with her honest Irish eyes, and said pathetically, "Please try to save him;" and went away. The following day she brought a sixth child in the same condition and learned of the death of the fifth. This child also died within a few hours, and the mother prayed earnestly that the remaining two of her flock might be spared.

Within a week, one after the other, the seventh and eighth children were brought to the hospital, past all hope; were operated upon, and died.

When the mother learned of this final tragedy, the poor, heartbroken woman reverently kissed the hand of the Doctor, who had unsuccessfully operated upon her eight children in a desperate attempt to save their lives:

"I have brought you the last one," she said simply. "There are no more. God bless you! "

FREQUENTLY patients, in whatever walk in life, seem to interpret the many questions asked by the Doctor as impertinent and needless. As an example of this, I remember an Irish laborer who was suffering from a severe blow on the head. In the course of taking his history, it was necessary to gain some idea of what sort of object struck him. Unfortunately, this question was not asked until some time had been consumed in gaining information regarding the patient's family and past history; and at this stage the Irishman's patience was about exhausted.

He stated, with a pronounced air of indifference, that he had been hit by a piece of wood about six feet long. When asked regarding the circumference of the piece of wood, he made a surly reply that if I would give him a tape-measure he would go and find out how large around it was.

It being obvious that our patient was getting into a peculiar frame of mind, I felt that he must be humored to gain the information I desired; so, holding up the pencil with which I was writing his history, I asked him if the piece of wood was as large around as the pencil, or more like one of the pillars in the ward, to which I pointed. Still sulky, he replied that he could not say. By this time, I was getting a bit impatient myself. I insisted that he give me the information I desired; and, holding up my finger by way of illustration, I asked him if the piece of wood was as large around as my finger, or as large around as my head.

He remained silent a moment, and then, sitting up in bed, he stretched forward toward me, applying his attention entirely to a careful observation, not of my finger, but of my head. Then, leaning back with an air of assurance and satisfaction, he remarked, "I think it was about as big around as your head; but it wasn't half so thick!"

A SIMILAR case was Mary Fogarty, an elderly Irish woman. She was not resentful, but she equally failed to cooperate with the interne who was attempting to get the history of her illness. The result of the interview proves the old saying that there is no defense against ignorance. It is also an example of how little help a doctor may receive in subjective investigation and explains why doctors so often consider objective findings the only basis for diagnosis and treatment.

When the interne asked this patient how old she was, she replied that she was about ten years older than her sister. An enquiry as to her sister's age led to the answer that her sister was, she thought, about a year older than her brother. No progress being made in this direction, the interne enquired as to how long she had been sick, her answer being, "Since about two years after Mother died"; and when asked how long-ago Mother died, she stated that Mother had never been well after

Father died. The only fact regarding Father's death that could be obtained was that he died after being ill for several years. Futile attempts to get any data in regard to these subjective matters led the interne to ask what the patient's trouble was. She enquired if he was a doctor, and, being assured of this fact, expressed the opinion that it was his job to find out what the matter was, as that was what she had come to the hospital to discover.

JAMES, in Bed 28, was a large, burly Irishman, admitted to the hospital because of a deformity in one of his big toes known to the profession as *Hallux Valgus*, and spoken of by the laity as a "bunion."

James, being unable to get brogans which would not make his daily toil as a street-cleaner miserable to a point of constant exclamation, had been advised by his friends to come to the hospital and see what might be done. It had been decided that an operation of a minor character should be performed, which promised entire relief to the annoying condition.

In making my morning visit, I was hailed by James, who said in his characteristic language,

"Shure, Docther, it's all off." "What's off, James?"

"Shure, the leg, sir. At least it was, but now thot I foind it on, I guess we'll lave it there."

James was much excited, and further questioning revealed the fact that during the night he had dreamed that, while being operated upon, he had suddenly come out of the ether, and had seen the ward-master disappearing with his whole leg tucked under his arm.

No explanation of mine could influence James as to our true intentions, and a few hours later found him hobbling with great speed and apparent fright out through the hospital gate.

JACK, "King of the Hobos," had met with an accident, and was taken to the Chronic Hospital, where he came under my charge. During a long convalescence, his irresponsible attitude towards life and his novel expressions were among the most interesting features of my daily routine. As we became better acquainted, I learned much regarding hobo life and of the Hobo Association.

This is an organization in which the members pay dues. So long as they are in good standing, they have access to records kept at headquarters, which are located in all large cities. From these they obtain information regarding places to sleep, means of travel, and where food may be obtained. Of course, in all walks of life there are easy officials guarding capital's interests, whose sympathies can be appealed to by the clever. Jack told me that if a member of the society wanted to go to San Francisco from New York, he would be provided with full information as to what trains could be jumped or worked through the sympathy of train-officials; what train-yards and buildings had watchmen who were sympathetic enough to extend the courtesy of a night's lodging; together with the names and addresses of people where food could be readily obtained by begging.

One day, while in conversation with Jack, he remarked that he was very grateful for all I had done for him, and that he would like to do something for me in return. I jocosely expressed my appreciation, but assured him that I had no intention of becoming a hobo, much as the life appealed to me. But Jack was serious. "Aren't you ever stopped in the street and touched for money?" he demanded.

Informing him that this was a common occurrence, he said,

"The next time this happens, you look the man straight in the eyes, and tell him that you have seen the blazing star."

I asked Jack if he really wanted to do me a good turn, or was trying to get me into trouble. He insisted that he was doing me a real service.

A few evenings later, having been to the theater, I was on my way home with a companion when a poorly dressed man stopped me and asked for money. What Jack had told me flashed into my mind, and, looking the beggar straight in the eye, as instructed, I said, in a very positive voice,

"I have seen the blazing star."

The beggar stepped back looking very much surprised. He took off his hat with some deference, and said, "I beg your pardon."

My friend and I continued on our way, and, as I glanced back, I saw the beggar still watching us. My friend was curious to know what it all meant and asked me where I had seen the blazing star. I told him that I was not quite certain, but that I would find out.

The following day, when I went to the hospital, I told Jack of my experience, and asked him what explanation he could offer for the beggar's conduct.

"Why," he explained, "he saw that you were well dressed and had the appearance of being a gentleman, so unquestionably said to himself,

"There is a *real* crook - one at the head of our profession!"

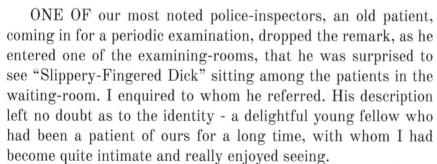

ONE OF our most noted police-inspectors, an old patient, coming in for a periodic examination, dropped the remark, as he entered one of the examining-rooms, that he was surprised to see "Slippery-Fingered Dick" sitting among the patients in the waiting-room. I enquired to whom he referred. His description left no doubt as to the identity - a delightful young fellow who had been a patient of ours for a long time, with whom I had become quite intimate and really enjoyed seeing.

While it is a principle not to discuss one patient with another, the inspector voluntarily, and with my interests at heart, informed me that Dick was the most skillful pickpocket in the business, - as he expressed it, "The slickest of them all." When this young man later made his appearance in one of the examining-rooms I ventured to remark that I had only recently learned of his skill with his hands. To this he immediately retorted with marked emphasis,

"So the 'Bull' has been roaring."

It would have been foolish to simulate that I did not know what a "Bull" might be, so, disregarding his insinuation, I expressed my admiration for those who used their hands skillfully, and truthfully paid compliment to the sleight-of-hand artist. To my sympathetic listener (and I understand that crooks are by necessity the best listeners) I allotted a high place in the practice of dexterity to the card-sharp, the dentist, and the pickpocket, and placed the surgeon as a technician far below others in the coordination of hand-training.

Vanity of accomplishment is usually cheered by such remarks as these and leads to confidence; but in this case my patient simply replied:

"That 'Bull' has bothered me for a long time. He's got me all mixed up with somebody else."

Of course, my job is to take care of patients' ills. Their social standing has nothing to do with my relations with them. The fact that people in various strata of society do me the honor to consult me about their physical defects is the only basis of our business relations. On the other hand, it is natural to extend to patients whatever mental support I can give during the time devoted to repairing their defects.

So it was that it became easy for me again to express my regret that he could not demonstrate to me the dexterity I so admired. He insisted that he was very clumsy with his hands, and he was sorry he did not possess the ability that the Inspector had attributed to him.

All this conversation took place while he was on a treatment-table, and I was standing nearby to do what was necessary. We were together only a few minutes. As he went out, I repeated my regret that he was not as clever as the Inspector had thought.

He had not been gone long, and I was about to see another patient when he returned to my private office. In his hand he held my watch, which I had worn on a chain passed through a buttonhole in my waistcoat, and a bunch of keys that I had carried in the side pocket of my trousers.

"Doctor," he remarked with a pleasant smile, "you tried to be so complimentary to me, and I like you so much, I thought that perhaps it might please you to have these articles back."

NATURALLY the Doctor who has to do with charity hospital-clinics comes in contact with bad characters as well as all other types. The respect that the criminal has for the Doctor is usually, I believe, of the most genuine sort.

During my obstetrical course I was living in the Lying-In Hospital located in the Boston slums. One night I received a call shortly after midnight, and as the distance was not great, went on foot, carrying my bag packed with the necessary paraphernalia to deliver a child. Crossing over the Dover Street bridge, which was deserted, I came to an alley at the other end. Here two men stepped out, each with a revolver. They demanded in the characteristic way of hold-ups that I "stick up my hands." One snatched the bag as I complied with the request, while the other started to go through my pockets.

Recovering from the first shock of the situation, I made the remark that I thought this was a fine piece of business on their part, to hold up a doctor who was on his way to help a poor woman who was about to have a child. The other man had opened the bag, and, hearing this remark, turned to his companion and said, "I guess this fellow's all right. The things in here look to me as if he is really a doctor." I assured him that I was, and that I was attached to the charity maternity-hospital and was really in a hurry to get to this woman who was in the process of having a child. Asking me where I was going, I told him. He said that he was sorry to have bothered me, but had no idea that I was a doctor. They had a horse and carriage in the alley, and at their invitation I got in and had a ride to the patient's house instead of going on foot as I had intended.

VI
OVERHEARD IN THE DOCTOR'S OFFICE

JOHN H CUNNINGHAM

A DOCTOR'S life touches so closely the depths of sorrow and tragedy that a sense of humor becomes absolutely imperative. This is by no means an evidence of lack of sympathy or of callousness. Unless the Doctor can hold himself reasonably impersonal in his association with his patients, his judgment might become of less value.

For my own interest I have jotted down, from time to time, incidents that have come to my attention not only in my own practice, but also in my association with my professional colleagues. Aside from their humorous aspect, some of these touch in an unusual way human notes with which we are all familiar, yet which we seldom hear sounded.

If the average layman were to spend an afternoon in a doctor's office, he would better understand some of the physician's problems, and perhaps realize that the doctor makes observations beyond those evident in the physical examinations.

DOCTOR GOODFELLOW was a little late in returning from his hospital clinic on this particular day, having been detained by a rather long list of operations, the last of which was most critical. Although he trusted absolutely in the ability of his house-surgeon, still he felt that he had better see it through himself.

The fact that his luncheon had consisted of a cup of chicken-broth and a few crackers, hurriedly consumed in the hospital dressing-room while changing his operating suit for the modest garb of a respected surgeon, made no visible difference to his good nature, and, as he called the first patient into the office from the crowded waiting-room, one might have believed that his morning had been spent casually knocking about a golf-ball, or in some other such trivial pastime.

The first patient who entered was a tall, well-built, middle-aged man, dressed in clothes of good texture, but without that indescribable ease of "hang" which characterizes one who has never worn any other sort. While some medical men are interested in determining the probable worldly possessions of the stranger who enters their offices, and how large a fee the patient will pay and not feel that he is being robbed, there are those who prefer to conjecture regarding the personal qualities of the stranger. Doctor Goodfellow was one of the latter class, and, from a few minutes' concrete reasoning, he had given his visitor a classification: his clothes, his weather-beaten face, and general manners, stamped him as a thrifty foreman engaged in some out-of-door occupation.

To one who usually finds himself right in his observations, there is a peculiar disappointment when the facts disprove the preliminary reasoning. By the same token, there is equal satisfaction when the facts confirm the analysis.

The Doctor's visitor opened his story by giving his name and history. After receiving his education as a civil engineer at Harvard, he had gone into the Northwest on a government survey. During the first year in this country, he had received a fracture of the hip, which kept him from work for several months. About the time when he was to resume his duty, he was persuaded by a half-breed to go into the Klondike, where he had found gold in fair amounts.

By this time Doctor Goodfellow questioned his original estimate, and hastened to correct it:

"Yes, yes, of course," he remarked, "you are a successful miner, and now go about with gold nuggets in your pockets."

The patient looked somewhat surprised at this diversion, but, after a moment's silence, continued his story: "Since my return to the East, a few weeks ago, the hip has been paining me at night. I want to find out what, if anything, is wrong with it."

An examination of the old injury was carefully made, and the Doctor prescribed definite treatment. While the patient was putting on his clothes the Doctor engaged him in conversation about life in general in the Klondike. The patient chatted about the large fortunes acquired by those who had gone early to this region, and the failure of those who had rushed there from all parts of the world, and from all walks of life, when the gold-fever was at its height. The genuine interest with which the Doctor listened and asked questions put the two men upon friendly terms.

The patient, having received instructions regarding the care of his hip, was about to leave the office, when, hesitating, he turned, and, looking the Doctor straight in the eye, said,

"How did you know I carried nuggets around in my pockets?"

The Doctor thought he would take a chance. He had noticed, while the patient was dressing, that there was an unusual bulge in the right hip-pocket of the man's trousers. Returning his pointed glance with equal frankness, the Doctor said smiling:

"Why, that is simple enough. It is quite obvious that you have some nuggets in your right hip-pocket."

The man laughed consciously. "Well," he said, "I'm glad everybody is not as observing as you, Doctor! Would you like to see them?" and he drew from his pocket a small canvas bag, in which were three large nuggets.

"You are certainly a mystery to me, Doctor. Here, you had better have this one. It has some quartz in it, but it will make you a novel paper-weight."

"A rather expensive one, my friend," remarked the Doctor.

"Perhaps," the patient agreed. "It is worth about two hundred and seventy-five dollars; but then, I have a few millions of those things they call dollars, and I want you to have this. So good-bye, Doctor. I don't understand how you found me out. I guess I will have to stand up against the buildings and cross my legs when I meet anyone on the street. Good-bye," and the office door closed.

THE DOCTOR was still smiling to himself when the waiting-room door was opened by the nurse, and in bustled a small, thin, high-strung woman who began to tell her story the moment she entered the room. Even so the Doctor instinctively classified her as from among the wealthy class, his estimate perhaps being influenced by the magnificent mink coat which covered obviously expensive clothing beneath.

"I don't think I could have stayed in that room one second longer," she exclaimed. "I thought that patient would never go. You know I'm not used to sitting still."

"Won't you be seated, madam?" was the courteous response as the new patient twisted herself into a chair, and began unbuttoning her gloves with as much haste as possible, at the same time rattling on:

"You know, Doctor, my stomach has been troubling me for so long. I never eat breakfast."

"Yes, madam. Please calm yourself, and we will talk your case over together."

"Well, you see, I must tell you all about it, and perhaps you can help me; but I don't think you can. So many doctors have tried."

"Then you have consulted a physician before?" "Well, I should say I had! There isn't a doctor in this city, or any other, that can understand my troubles. Doctor Nervine told me I had nervous dyspepsia, and Doctor Learned said it was—something, I don't know what; and Doctor—"

"Yes; madam. How many doctors have you seen?" "How many? I guess I have seen every doctor worth seeing in this city, and none of them ever did me any good. There isn't one of them that understands my case half as well as I do myself." "Do you expect me to help you?"

"I don't know. I should think that somebody would understand my case. Other people seem to get cured of their troubles; but then, I don't suppose anyone was ever as bad off as I am."

"The doctors that you name, madam, are all excellent men. How many times did you go to them?" "I went to Dr. Nervine twice in two months; to Dr. Learned once, and to Dr. Brilliant once, and—" "You don't seem to have stayed with any doctor very long."

"No, I guess I didn't. They didn't help me. The only thing that helped me was some medicine I got at the apothecary store, and I didn't have to pay for a doctor's advice either. I read about it in the newspaper."

"Yes, madam. I think that medicine which you mention is just what you need. I cannot give you anything better, or half so good. I recommend you take it regularly."

"Do you mean to say that you can't cure me right off quick?"

"I think that the medicine you mentioned is what you need, and you know I must see the other patients who are waiting."

"Well, can you tell me what the name of it is? I have forgotten."

"I think your druggist will remember, madam." "Perhaps he will; but he's so stupid. Dear me! How late it is! I must hurry home. My husband has been away for two whole days on business, and promised to be back last night, and I wonder if he has come yet. How much do I owe you, Doctor? I don't see that you are any better than the others. You can't charge more than a dollar," and she counted out some silver and pennies, and laid them on a chair.

"I hope I shall never see another doctor as long as I live," she remarked as she jammed her hand into one of the gloves from which she had picked the finger tips during her long talk.

"Good day, madam "; and the Doctor quietly closed the door which he had held open for at least a minute, while the lively invalid adjusted her hat, arranged her veil, dusted her skirt, fixed her neckwear, and tied her shoe-strings a little tighter.

A DOCTOR-FRIEND of mine attained fame as a baby doctor far beyond his expectations, and also beyond what he could reasonably hope to maintain. Possessing a rather whimsical personality, he early formed the habit of asking the expectant mother of which sex she wished her child to be. On receiving her answer, he would very gravely enter the facts in his notebook:

"This is all a matter of diet," he would remark with seeming seriousness. "The fulfillment of your desire depends upon the fidelity with which you carry out: my instructions."

Not being an expectant mother himself, he did not realize at first how seriously his patient rested upon his assurances. He prescribed a well-balanced diet, always referred to the coming child as a boy or a girl as the promise might have been, and by an extraordinary run of luck scored an almost perfect record.

The Doctor's reputation increased by leaps and bounds. New patients confided to him that they came to him because they were so particularly anxious concerning the sex of the coming child. He soon realized that what had been started as a passing pleasantry had become a serious liability. The question of sex is a 50-50 proposition, and the good fortune the Doctor had already enjoyed simply increased the percentage against him.

Something had to be done about it, so the Doctor put on his thinking-cap; and his ingenuity proved equal to the emergency.

When a disappointed mother took him to task he made every show of being completely surprised:

"What's that?" he would enquire, drawing his notebook from his pocket. "Either you have forgotten, or I stupidly made a mistake in my entry."

Then he would show her the book, turning to the page on which her name appeared:

"Confinement about September first. Wants a girl. Girl diet prescribed. Impression is that mother will be faithful to diet."

"There - you see?" he would exclaim triumphantly. "Could you have made a—or could I have misunderstood you? You certainly could not get a boy with my girl diet!"

IN HIS own home, the Doctor took no such chances. His wife was naturally of a querulous disposition - a condition which increased during the months of her pregnancy. She seemed to take peculiar delight in trying to humiliate her husband during meal-time, much to the unvoiced indignation of the servants, who adored the Doctor.

At breakfast one morning she was particularly cantankerous, but the Doctor refused to let himself become annoyed. During the meal he tried in vain to pacify her, and finally left for his office with a good-natured admonition to be calm. Exasperated by her failure to arouse some antagonism in her husband, she turned her spleen on the surprised and innocent waitress. This was the final spark to bring on a long-delayed explosion:

"So that's what ye think, is it, ma'am? "Nora cried out indignantly. "Then I'll be tellin' ye I won't be workin' for the likes of ye no more. A wife like ye that don't know when she has a grand, noble husband, is no lady. I've only stayed on any way to help the dear Doctor -"

"You are discharged" her mistress declared, outraged by her impertinence.

"Shure I'm discharged. I've discharged me'self. An' I'm hopin' that when yer son is born ye'll suffer plenty."

Curiosity overcame indignation for a moment:
"Why are you so sure I'm going to have a son, Nora?" The maid tossed her head defiantly. "Shure ye ought to know that as well as me - no *girl* would be stayin' wid yer for nine months!"

PROFESSOR DOUGLAS LITHGOW was among the most noted ethnologists of his time. His knowledge of the American Indian, gained in large part by living among many tribes, had made him perhaps the outstanding authority on this subject, and when with his friends in ethnological gatherings he was always referred to as "Indian Doug."

This learned gentleman had always insisted that he had a great advantage over most of his other professorial friends, who, he would remark, gleaned their knowledge from the library, while he lived mostly in the field with the most healthy, normal-living people in America. This was a theme that he enjoyed to elaborate, and he would, on all occasions, ref er to his state of physical well-being and his freedom from the maladies that would later attack his associates who lived the sedentary life.

Some of his friends did not accept all that he said about the advantages of the "natural" life he led. They predicted that, sooner or later, he would suffer some severe illness, and, being away from civilization, would probably die before he could receive medical care, while they, living in the midst of civilization and culture, would receive such benefits immediately. This discussion was the source of much amusement among them when the Professor made his periodical returns to civilization.

The prognostication of the Professor's friends finally came true. While in a desert country the Professor suddenly felt a terrible pain in his back, and, while he applied the time-honored Indian remedies, he suffered such agony that he was unable to move. After several days of jouncing on an improvised stretcher, he arrived at a small western hospital. Here it was discovered that he had a stone in the right kidney. Receiving temporary relief, he returned to the center of learning, where his academic friends received him with kindly feelings but not altogether sympathetic remarks.

The offending stone was removed from his kidney, and, believe it or not, this stone had the peculiarity of being exactly the shape and size of the common type of Indian arrowhead. One of the Professor's friends remarked that if intensive study so saturated one with the object of his investigations, he was going to become a lapidary!

SPEAKING of cats reminds me of an incident that occurred during one of my annual duck-hunting trips to Currituck Sound. It was necessary to stop over in Norfolk for several hours in the middle of the day to make a train connection. On this occasion my companion, Dr. Frank Hagner, and I were invited to lunch at a club with an old friend of ours, Judge Jim Goude, who was President of the club at that time. The Judge had invited several of our mutual friends to be with us, and, while we were having lunch, a large cat wandered in and began rubbing up against the Judge's leg.

Doctor Hagner, always full of practical jokes and good humor, upon noticing the cat said to our host, "Why, Jim, I see you have a mustard cat here." When the Judge asked him what he meant, Frank replied that this particular kind of cat ate mustard. The Judge was incredulous, insisting that the cat had been around the club for a long time, and he had no reason to believe that it would eat mustard.

There was a good deal of arguing about the matter, and finally Frank bet the Judge ten dollars that this cat would eat mustard. A waiter was ordered to bring a pot of mustard for the experiment. Frank, holding the cat in his lap, took a daub of mustard on the wooden spatula from the mustard-pot, and, lifting the cat's tail, deposited it beneath the tail on the anal outlet. The cat was then put on the floor, where it immediately began to lap the irritant, and Frank coolly collected the ten dollars, much to the amusement of the group.

Shortly after returning home, with this episode still in mind, I was one evening with a group of friends enjoying cocktails at a club-bar, when a friend joined us leading a fair sized bulldog. Being in a jocose frame of mind, normally or artificially produced by the libations, I greeted my friend with the dog, and remarked that I saw that his dog was a mustard dog. The same reaction followed as with the Judge, as to whether or not the dog would eat mustard, the owner insisting that he would not.

A bet having been made, the mustard-pot and spoon were brought, and the condiment applied beneath the dog's tail. The beast took one look at me and then sank his teeth in the calf of my leg.

As far as I know, the mustard is still under the dog's tail. At any rate, I lost the bet, my one consolation being that my friend's pet was a dog rather than a lion or some other more ferocious beast. I needed no further argument to persuade me that what works with cats does not, apparently, always work with dogs.

FORTUNATELY, not everyone holds views on the medical profession which Bernard Shaw expressed in his "Doctor's Dilemma" - a scurrilous satire which is destructive with no constructive compensation. Its humor is characteristically brilliant, and, except for the fact that it disturbs the confidence which the average laymen rightly feel in the medical profession, there would be no occasion to subject it to criticism. On the other hand, there are some laymen whose reliance on a doctor's statement is far too absolute.

Years ago, during the month of April, a Jewish gentleman consulted me in regard to a hernia. After it was decided to have an operation, and upon receiving assurance that delay would not be important, the man announced that he would like to have it performed on the seventh day of June. By way of explanation, he added that his reason for picking this date was that his brother was going to die on the first day of June.

This statement rather startled me, as June first was some two months in the future. I asked the man how he knew that his brother was going to die on that particular date, and jocosely expressed my hope that this was not a case of premeditated murder or legal execution. My patient was much disturbed by my levity. "My brother has been ill for a long time," he explained gravely. "After several consultations, the Professor Doctor saw my brother with his regular physician, and they told me that my brother would live six months. The six months will be up on June first."

Such confidence in members of the medical profession as exact scientists is heartening, and it would be interesting to learn Shaw's comment upon this state of mind.

SOMETIMES, it must be confessed, a doctor's point of view depends a good deal upon his surroundings and his personal feelings. If one consults a doctor after he has just eaten a good meal, the patient is very likely to be told that he will have to go on a restricted diet; but if the Doctor himself happens to be hungry, he is more inclined to prescribe food.

I recall an anecdote that went the rounds concerning Dr. Franz Pfaff, who was a very domineering Swiss physician, at one time the vogue in Boston in connection with stomach troubles. He received at his office every morning, to have their stomachs washed out, a great many patients who consistently over-ate. A friend of mine told me one day that he had met the Doctor in the Club one evening, after having been in his office as a patient not more than two hours previously. He spoke to him, and the Doctor said genially:

"How do you do? I am very glad to see you. We will now haff a little drink together."

The patient replied: "Doctor, you evidently do not remember me. When I was in your office this afternoon, you told me that if I drank any more liquor, it would kill me."

"Did I say that?" asked Doctor Pfaff. Then, after a moment's hesitation, he continued: "But that was in my office. This is in the Club. We vill now go and haff our little drink."

~

A DOCTOR-FRIEND, while modern in many things in life, still held to the old-fashioned custom of sleeping in a double-bed with his wife. He had instructed her, in their early married life, to answer the telephone when it rang after they had retired, realizing from his experience as a bachelor that he often became involved with unimportant night-calls which might just as well have been postponed until the following day. When a night-call came in, his wife would answer the telephone, enquire who it was, and relay the information, so that the Doctor might decide whether or not he wished to take over the conversation himself. Her prescribed method was to ask who it was, and then say,

"Hold the line, and I will see if the Doctor has come in yet."

On one occasion this reply was made without looking at the clock. The patient exclaimed, "What? It is after three o'clock in the morning, and if the Doctor is in the habit of staying out all night, perhaps I had better get another doctor whose habits are better."

On another occasion the wife, answering the telephone in the usual manner, passed the message on to her husband, who was half-asleep in the bed. He did not wish to converse with this patient, a nervous woman who frequently annoyed him about quite unimportant matters at any time of day or night. So, he asked his wife to enquire what the trouble was. The lady replied that her husband was in distress, and she wished the Doctor to come immediately to see him. This the Doctor did not wish to do without additional information, so he urged his wife to enquire further in regard to the husband's difficulty. Getting this information, and again passing it on to her husband, the wife was instructed to tell the lady that the Doctor was out, but that the situation would be explained to him when he returned.

"This is really quite awkward," retorted the voice on the telephone. "I am much disturbed about my husband. As the Doctor is out, I wonder if the man in bed with you could give me some advice."

THE HONORABLE community of the laity does not realize that money-making by conniving is a highly developed profession. Doctors, especially those interested in the insurance aspects of medicine; could write volumes upon this subject. My colleague, Dr. Edmund Saunders, as a young man was fortunate in obtaining a position in the medical department of one of our large insurance companies in which he learned many things that are not ordinarily included in the practice of medicine.

On one occasion a claim was made against one of our best restaurants, which was turned over to the insurance company, and thus came to Doctor Saunders for investigation. A man claimed that, while eating a chicken-pie, he not only masticated but actually swallowed a cockroach, and in consequence had become violently ill. He sued the restaurant, and his claim was substantiated by a doctor of questionable medical standing.

Doctor Saunders examined the patient for the Company, attended by the fake doctor. At an opportune moment, the claimant's doctor, in a confidential undertone, informed Doctor Saunders that as the restaurant carried a policy to cover just such matters, he hoped that he would use his influence to secure a substantial settlement. He did not point out, however, what Doctor Saunders well knew, that if the malingerer did not get a settlement, the fake doctor would go without his fee. While Doctor Saunders found absolutely nothing the matter with the plaintiff, the insurance company made a small settlement as the simplest way of disposing of the matter.

Doctor Saunders later became medical-examiner in another company. In the regular routine, he was asked to examine, for this new company, an individual who claimed to have become ill from eating a cockroach in one of our best restaurants. The claimant proved to be the same individual, attended by the same doctor as before; but it was a different restaurant.

This time Doctor Saunders influenced the Company to take the claim to court. As a result of their investigation, evidence was received that this man had "worked" most of the big cities of the East with this same trick. He always picked restaurants of high standing and had made twelve claims of being made ill by eating cockroaches during a period of five years. He was known in his· profession as "Cockroach Charlie," and was in such good standing that his fellow-malingerers never encroached upon his cockroach racket.

WHEN a Jewish person is to be operated upon, there is usually quite a congregation of relatives and friends awaiting the surgeon after the operation has been completed. In most instances they are desirous of seeing what the surgeon has removed. Just what prompts this curiosity is, of course, a question. Perhaps it is to be sure that they get what they are paying for.

However, this may be, I once removed a stone from a Jewish friend's kidney, and, realizing that the family would probably wish to see the object, I had it with me when I joined the group assembled in the hospital waiting-room. After assuring them of the patient's good condition and answering the usual enquiries peculiar to this race on such occasions, I was asked by the son if he could inspect the stone.

Anticipating this request, I had carefully washed the stone to make it more presentable, and the son, taking it in his hand and presenting it to the enquiring gaze of those assembled, asked me if it was genuine. I explained that in composition it differed from such stones as might be found in the garden or on the beach, but it was nevertheless a real stone.

"What I want to know," said the son insistently, "is whether or not this is a *genuine* stone."

"Yes," I replied, "it is certainly a genuine stone." "Well," remarked the son; "I have been in the jewelry business with my father for many years, and this is the first genuine stone that Father has ever had."

I ONCE had a curious experience with a patient who was brought to me by a colleague with a malady which required a surgical operation. The patient finally admitted that he did not dare to have the operation performed. Just why he was so cowardly he could not explain, but the thought of going to the hospital terrified him. His doctor brought him back to me on several occasions, as his condition was getting progressively worse. Each time the man stated that he wished he could make up his mind to have the operation done, but simply could not.

At last, the patient said that he had thought out a means which would force him to have the operation. He explained that there was perhaps only one thing he valued as much as his life, and that was his money. The loss of any money upset him so much that he felt that the best way to bring himself to do what he should for his health was to pay me for the operation then and there. We discussed the figure, and he gave me my fee. I made all the arrangements at the hospital for him to enter and have the operation performed.

This occurred some fifteen or twenty years ago, and I have never seen or heard from this man since!

I HAD another patient, who made a somewhat similar mysterious disappearance, but not because of cowardice. This man had a chronic ailment which disturbed him but little excepting for the nervous state of mind into which he had gotten in consequence of having it. There was scarcely a day over a period of months that he did not telephone me, describing some unimportant symptom. Even after paying a visit at my office, it was his custom to ring up soon afterwards and tell me how the treatment had affected him. His frequent messages became part of the daily expectations.

It was discovered quite accidentally that he had a tapeworm, and I gave him full directions about taking a vermifuge. The instructions in regard to his catharsis and the taking of the medicine to cure the worm were carefully written out for him and explained. He left the office, and, after getting the medicine at the drugstore, called m-e up to say that he had secured it, and was about to go home and take it. This did not surprise me, but the next day he did not telephone as usual, although I had expected a report of just how the medicine was performing. In fact, I have never heard from him since.

REPUTATIONS in the medical profession are sometimes achieved in a curious way. I was once invited to attend a large medical-congress in Kansas City and deliver a paper before that gathering. The invitation conveyed the information that all expenses would be paid, and that the committee would be glad to arrange plans for my entertainment.

As I have always been an enthusiast on duck-shooting and have never had the opportunity to shoot ducks in the cornfields of Kansas, this offered an experience I had always wished to have. So, it was arranged that after the Kansas City medical-meeting I was to be personally conducted to "the best duck-shooting in the West" by another doctor, who was equally an enthusiast, and who knew all the ropes.

The plan was carried out, and I enjoyed not only the duck-shooting but the generous hospitality of a Doctor Trueheart- a gentleman who was most appropriately named.

One day, after an early morning shoot, Doctor Trueheart enquired if it would be an imposition to ask me to take a look at an old lady at a farm on the way home, saying that when it had been learned by these people that a doctor from Harvard was staying with him, they had urgently requested that he be called in consultation.

Of course, I willingly acquiesced. He then told me that the patient, an elderly German lady, wife of one of the richest farmers in that district, was critically ill with stomach-disease; in fact, so ill that as her doctor he had decided that nothing surgical could be done with safety. The outlook was extremely bad, and all the doctors who had seen her agreed that she would die soon unless she could be made to retain some food. I found myself welcomed by the assembled family and friends as a sort of Messiah and was taken by Doctor Trueheart to the patient. After sensing the situation, and making the necessary examination, I told them quite truthfully that I agreed with all that Doctor Trueheart had said and done, and that it would be a miracle if the patient recovered.

The eldest daughter had remained with her mother after I had left her room. Joining the group while we were still in conversation, she asked if the "nice doctor would return, as Mother likes him and wishes to ask him a question." Returning to the old lady, she told me of the comfort she had received from my visit, and asked why it was she could not be given to eat the things she enjoyed most. I asked what it was she had in mind. The old lady feebly said:

"They feed me only on the poorest kind of food - milk, eggs, and all kinds of new-fangled preparations. If I could only have some beer and sauerkraut I would get well. Nobody can get well eating the sort of food that they feed me. Please, Doctor, use your influence to get me what I know will cure me."

Returning to the family group, I repeated what the patient had said.

"Why not give her what she wants?" I suggested. "She can't be saved. It is all the same in the end."

Doctor Trueheart agreed that to grant this request could not damage a lost cause. Returning to the patient, I informed her that Doctor Trueheart and I had discussed the matter, and that she could have the beer and sauerkraut if it was to be had.

The old lady exclaimed, "To be had! We have hogsheads of sauerkraut in the cellar, just mixed this fall; and as for beer, we have barrels of it always."

I soothed the patient with the statement that if she liked she could eat all the hogsheads of sauerkraut and drink all the barrels of beer. This remark was overheard by those assembled in the outer room, and some frowned on me as I left the patient still expressing her heartfelt thanks. So it was that we duck-shooting doctors went home to breakfast. The next day I left for the East, having had a most delightful experience not only from the duck-shooting, but also from other expressions of hospitality on the part of Doctor Trueheart. The following year I was fortunate in meeting Doctor Trueheart at a medical-meeting in the East. After enquiring about the duck-shooting, I asked casually how long the old German lady had lived. Much to my surprise, I was told that she was still alive.

"You ruined my practice," Doctor Trueheart said, laughing. "Your reputation still abides. The whole country about thinks that I am a washed-out physician, and that they would all live forever if you would establish yourself among them. In fact, everybody now takes beer and sauerkraut for all complaints, and you have not only gotten me in bad repute, but many are dying from this notion you have given them."

This was, of course, a bit of exaggeration, but the fact remains that the old German lady is still alive fifteen years after this episode and is now ninety years old. Moreover, she insists that the Doctor from the Harvard Medical School is the greatest doctor in the world!

A FRIEND of mine, Dr. Frank Watson, was not so fortunate in combining medicine with duck-shooting. On an occasion when he was going to Cape Cod on a gunning-trip, he had a basket of black-duck decoys that he intended to take with him. When he went out to lunch, he felt the ducks would be more comfortable if he let them out of their confinement. As they needed a bit of fresh air, he opened the window over his sign for an inch or so and left the ducks to waddle about the room until he returned.

As he approached his office, on his return from lunch, he noticed quite a gathering of people in front of his window, who seemed to be enjoying themselves hugely. As he came nearer, he discovered that several of the ducks had their heads stuck out through the slightly-opened window, shouting "Quack" directly over his sign!

To preserve his self-respect, he rushed in and ended this questionable notoriety by closing the window on the necks of the ducks. Since then he has done his best to live down the reputation these birds gave him.

MEDICAL fees, especially those of the surgeon, concern not only the patients but the doctor, and the manner of handling the subject has been given much consideration from many angles. I am among those who believe that the matter of fee is one to be arranged to the satisfaction of the patient rather than arbitrarily. My attitude has always been that anyone choosing me as his surgeon paid me a compliment; that my duty was to get the patient well if it lay in my power; and that the patient's duty was only to pay a fee which was consistent with his financial position.

I have always believed in the theory, commonly expressed by blunt politicians, that people are born "free and equal" in the U.S.A., but, so far as I can see, such an equality has no lasting quality except when "under the knife." Here the wealthy and the pauper receive the same technical skill of the surgeon, and the only just basis of remuneration is what the individual patient desires to give in recognition of the surgeon's service, and his ability to express such appreciation.

This principle of doing my professional best for the individual patient and expecting the patient to do his best for me, has led to many conversations in regard to the matter of fees, and has created a large circle of friends. One day a patient, upon whom I had operated, remarked that he had received no bill, and that he was • prepared to pay. The dialogue that ensued was somewhat as follows:

Doctor. "I don't know your circumstances. What amount would seem right to you?"

Patient. "Naturally that question is difficult for me to answer. I have no idea what you charge for such an operation."

Doctor. "I have no set charge. My job was to get you well, and your job is to pay me what you can without financial embarrassment. I want you to be entirely satisfied."

Patient. "I'll gladly tell you what I earn and what I have saved."

Doctor. "Really that is not important. There may be many demands upon the results of your industry." The patient still insisted that I name his fee. At last I compromised:

"I will name a sum if you will frankly say whether or not it is satisfactory. Suppose we call it $1000. Do you think that is about right?"

Patient. "No."

Doctor. "$900?"

Patient. "No." *Doctor.* "$800?" *Patient.* "No." *Doctor.* "$500?" *Patient.* "No." *Doctor.* "Nothing." *Patient.* "No."

Doctor (smiling). "Well, I can't go any lower."

Patient. "You said I could name my own price, as I understand it."

Doctor. "Correct."

Patient. "I say $2500. I only wish I were able to make it more."

So it is that the patient does not always want to "chisel." In applying the method, I have always found more difficulty in persuading patients that they are trying to pay too much than not enough. I still believe in human nature and am convinced that a conscience is the best thing that man possesses.

AN ELDERLY gentleman, with a complaint common to the male of advanced years, had been referred to me. As a result of the physical examination, the patient was told a surgical operation was the only means of relieving his difficulty. To this he agreed, stating that he had received the same advice from noted men in England, France, Germany, and in other cities in this country.

It being accepted that the operation was necessary, the patient enquired as to my fee. As was my usual custom, I stated that I would charge him an amount agreeable to him; knowing nothing of his circumstances, the matter of the fee must remain in his hands to decide. The man objected to any such arrangement in no uncertain terms, and expressed his surprise that I had no fixed charge for the operation under consideration.

I tried to explain that I could have no fixed charge that what could be easily paid by one person might be an impossible burden for another. This explanation failed to prove convincing. The patient made some rather caustic remarks about my method of doing business.

"I am a glue-merchant," he stated. "Anybody who enquires from me the price of a carload of glue gets it to the cent, and he can take it or leave it."

I tried to explain that I was not dealing in merchandise that one might buy at one price and sell at another - that what I had to sell was knowledge, experience, and skill. Still, the glue-merchant was dissatisfied. Finally, he said:

"Doctor, if you have a price for this operation, tell me what it is. If you have not, I will have to go somewhere else, which I am reluctant to do. I can't do business by your method, which is really wasting my time and is no method at all."

I finally became disgusted by the man's commercial attitude, and to end the matter said, "All right, I will operate on a glue basis. My price is $10,000. Take it or leave it."

"I'll take it," said the glue-merchant, much to my surprise, for I thought the sum mentioned would relieve me of his presence.

There is a second chapter to this episode. During the patient's stay in the hospital, the merchant and I became better acquainted, and I received much free advice regarding the way I should conduct the business side of my profession. I made myself a good listener, and while admitting, for argument's sake, that perhaps the merchant was right, in reality I adhered to my conviction that commercial methods could not be introduced into the practice of surgery.

A few years after the glue-merchant had left the hospital, he again called on me and enquired if any change had been made in my method of doing business. I replied in the negative. To my surprise, this seemed to cheer the glue-merchant.

"I'm glad you didn't take my advice," he said cheerfully. "My daughter has a stone in her kidney. I want you to operate, and if you fixed your price the way I fix the price of glue, I never could afford to pay you!"

The occasion for his remark was soon apparent. The merchant had retired from the glue-business a rich man, but change of economic conditions had reduced his estate. This time, without his former bluster, he enquired if I would do the operation, and what the fee would be. I smiled as I reminded him that I had no fixed fee for that operation, as I intended always to make my charge consistent with the patient's financial circumstances.

"Will you do it for $500?" the man asked anxiously.

"That's the price," I replied. "You know what is right, and I don't. I'll be fair with you, and I feel sure you are being fair with me."

"Yes, Doctor. I have learned much about your profession since I first came to you all stuck up with my 'glue-money.'"

I must confess to a degree of satisfaction in this demonstration of what most surgeons in all parts of our country realize - that the only real defense against capitalizing the distress of physical ailments is the unsurmountable obstacle of having the instincts of a gentleman. The absence of this instinct explains the success of the "Department Store Surgery," as a titled English surgeon once called it, and the ability of the charlatan to prey on the unfortunate.

ABOUT 1920 not only the medical profession but all the world was greatly interested in the wonders being accomplished by the use of radium in curing ailments which had been considered surgically too severe or too difficult to be handled. I had been interested in this medium and its therapeutic use for some time before it came to be generally known and had been fortunate enough to acquire a small amount of the priceless element. Some of my colleagues knew that I possessed this, and, while realizing that my interest in connection with radium was in deep-seated tumor-growths rather than in skin-lesions, they nevertheless occasionally requested me to employ it in certain skin-conditions affecting their own patients.

One of my friends consulted me one afternoon, bringing with him as patient a man eighty years old - a cultivated gentleman in possession of all his faculties. He had a growth about the size of a silver dollar on his right fore-arm, and his physician, noting the parchment-like appearance of the skin, had an idea that the removal of the growth by surgery might result in a slow-healing process because of the lack of nutrition in the skin. He therefore wished to secure the benefit of my opinion as to the treatment of this skin-cancer by radium.

I agreed that radium would be the most suitable treatment, and the capsule containing the element was applied to the growth. In the treatment it was necessary for the patient to sit in one of my rooms for perhaps an hour while the radium was being applied. During this period, he kept up a running conversation with me, remarking, for instance, that he felt no sensation from the treatment; to which I replied that there would be no sensation. He assured me that what was being done would be of absolutely no benefit, and my assurances that after a few treatments the growth would disappear were received with amused incredulity. He declared that the whole thing was nothing but buncombe, and the only reason that he continued to accept it was because he had had much experience in sizing up men, and I did not seem to be one who would be guilty of deliberate deception.

After still further treatments, the patient varied his attack by offering to make a bet with me. When I refused to enter into this, the patient declared that I was simply sidestepping, and that he began to think I was a buncombe after all. All this bantering was, of course, good-natured. I was frankly amused by the incredulity of the patient, even when he continued to insist that he wanted to put up any part of a thousand dollars that, no matter how many treatments were given him, they would have no influence upon the skin cancer.

I succeeded in jollying my patient along so that he continued to receive the treatments in spite of his insistence upon their lack of value. At last, the number of treatments originally decided upon had been applied, with no outward change in the appearance of the growth. I told my patient not to return for two months, as it would require that length of time for the radium to accomplish the results I confidently expected.

At the end of this period the old gentleman returned to the office. When I received him, he rolled up his sleeve, and with no comment presented his arm for inspection. The growth had entirely disappeared. Greatly relieved, but with the idea of continuing to play the game, I said,

"You have rolled up the wrong sleeve. What I want to see is the arm with the growth on it."

"This is the right arm," the patient insisted.

"I know that it is the right arm," I retorted; "but I want to see the left. The left is right."

"No," said the patient, "the right is right." After this merry piece of repartee, the old gentleman said seriously:

"Doctor, of course I am pleased to have this growth disappear, but I am even more delighted to discover that you are not a buncombe after all. When you applied that capsule which produced no sensation, and refused to bet with me, I was really convinced that, for the first time in my life, appearances were deceitful. Don't bother to render me a bill. Here is my check for $1,000.

"But that is much more than I should have charged you," I exclaimed.

"But I was only too ready to bet you a thousand dollars," the patient insisted. "If I had bet, I should have lost that amount, so you are fully entitled to it. As a matter of fact, I think you are entitled to more because of my error in misjudging your character."

IMPOSITION is sometimes met by doctors beyond the matter of fees. A young man came to a doctor's office about ten o'clock one evening while it was storming, and enquired what the Doctor's charge would be to go out to his house, which was some distance in the country. The Doctor said it would be the usual charge of $5.00, to which the young man agreed.

When they arrived at the house indicated, the young man paid the Doctor the $5.00 and thanked him for bringing him out. The Doctor, surprised, demanded what the idea was in paying him before he saw the patient.

"There is no patient," the young man informed him. "At the garage, they would not bring me out here for less than $10.00. I enquired your price and consider your offer of $5.00 very moderate!"

A SIMILAR experience is recorded in the case-book of another doctor, who lived in a community in which there were many Scotch folk. He was called one night into the country, and, arriving at the patient's home, knocked on the door. The owner of the house opened a second-story window, and, putting his head out, asked the Doctor what he was going to charge to come in to see his sick wife.

"Three dollars," the Doctor told him.

"Too much," was the reply. "It's nae worth it!" and the window slammed.

ANOTHER Scotch story is of a Scotchman who once consulted a noted physician about a rather indefinite physical condition, which required considerable conversation in regard to symptoms, and much time in making examinations. The Physician outlined very carefully all the details that the patient should observe. As the Scotchman was leaving with no suggestion of paying the fee, the Doctor casually remarked, "You know, I usually receive a guinea for my advice."

To this the patient replied, "Quite so; but I am not going to take your advice."

THIS is a story with a Boccaccian flavor. I had made a special study of a rather rare kidney-disease, to the surgical treatment of which I had made certain contributions. My writings on this subject attracted enough attention to give me the privilege of operating upon many of these cases. The material for study, because of the rarity of the disease, was greatly prized and sought after, and every specimen that I could obtain was not only photographed but painted in colors, as well as being carefully studied under the microscope. This particular kidney-disease is an acute condition requiring an emergency operation.

I was called in consultation late one night by a physician who suspected the condition in which I was interested. The physician's diagnosis was correct, and an operation for the removal of the kidney was completed in the early hours of the morning. The specimen was an unusually good one, and upon arriving home, I placed the kidney, carefully wrapped in gauze with certain solutions, in my ice-chest, with the intention of taking it to the laboratory in the morning and having it carefully recorded, as I had done with my other specrmens.

At breakfast I was served with a dish which was not familiar to me, but which I particularly enjoyed. Enquiring of the maid what it was, I was told that it was the package which the cook had found in the icechest and presumed I desired to have prepared for breakfast. As it was my habit occasionally to bring some special delicacy home with me, for the cook's later culinary attention, I could find no fault, but at least I could express my regret that this particular specimen could not be included among the others in my collection. I think I am entitled to the distinction of being the only cannibal in captivity!

PRACTICAL jokes sometimes lead to embarrassing situations, as may be illustrated by the following story in which a Washington friend of mine, Dr. Frank Hagner, was the victim. Doctor Hagner was a confirmed practical joker, and his friends were always awaiting the opportunity to pay him back for some of the pranks which he has perpetrated on them. This opportunity came when the Russian and Japanese delegations arrived in Washington, at the invitation of President Theodore Roosevelt, on their way to the Peace Conference to be held in Portsmouth, New Hampshire.

One of Doctor Hagner's prevailing characteristics was a peculiar aversion to the telephone. When he had to make use of it, his first reaction was to demand in a very irritable way just why he was being called. About one o'clock in the morning of the day after the Russian delegation arrived, Doctor Hagner was awakened by the ringing of his telephone. The Doctor made use of a sleeping-porch, so to reach the telephone he was put to considerable inconvenience. In his characteristic manner he bellowed,

"Hello! What do you want?"

A polite response came that the speaker was Baron Rosen, a member of the Russian Delegation. Continuing, he said that when he left St. Petersburg, Doctor Kowski had advised him, if he had any necessity to call a physician, to put himself in the hands of Doctor Hagner. He regretted inconveniencing the Doctor, particularly at this hour of the morning, but he was in great distress and would appreciate an immediate call.

Doctor Hagner's attitude at once changed. He found that the Baron was installed at the New Willard and assured him that he would call upon him as soon as he could get there. He got out his car and ran over to his office, where he secured such surgical paraphernalia as he thought might be necessary, and then presented himself at the New Willard Hotel. On his arrival he found a group of his friends awaiting him in the lobby. He at once realized that the call had been a hoax, and the amusement expressed by his friends did not serve to mollify his resentment.

A few weeks later, just after midnight, Doctor Hagner was again forced to go to the telephone. Answering it in the same characteristic surly manner, he was informed that the White House was on the line, and that President Roosevelt wished him to come right over. The Doctor at once scented another practical joke, and curtly replied,

"Tell the President to go to hell," and rang off.

It so happened that President Roosevelt was an intimate friend of the Doctor's, and, in fact, the Doctor's sister, Belle, was at that very time Mrs. Roosevelt's social secretary. For years the Roosevelt and Hagner families had been on intimate terms, and the President looked to the Doctor for advice considerably beyond that expected from a medical consultant.

The Doctor returned to his cot on the porch, and again the telephone rang. At first, he paid no attention to it, but the persistency forced him to answer it. Thoroughly exasperated, he took the receiver off the hook and began to express his opinion, when he recognized President Roosevelt's voice. The President enquired if it was true that he had told him to go to hell, adding that, as a matter of fact, he really needed professional advice, and, if it fitted in with the Doctor's plans, he would like to postpone his journey to the infernal regions until after they had had a conference. Doctor Hagner apologized abjectly, and presented himself promptly at the White House, but the double success of their practical joke was not overlooked by the Doctor's many friends.

A CERTAIN doctor, who was one of the greatest authorities on children's diseases, being professor of pediatrics in the University, was one night entertaining as guests at dinner a very distinguished group of American and foreign doctors, interested in his specialty. He had instructed the butler that he was not to be disturbed during the evening except in some case of life or death, and the butler was to use his intelligence to dispose of any call that might come in.

The Doctor had planned a sumptuous dinner, perfect in detail, culminating in a succession of rare vintages which were so highly appreciated by his guests that the host felt obliged to indulge himself to an unusual extent.

While the party was at its height, and much to the Doctor's surprise, the butler ushered in a friend who seemed to be very much perturbed and who engaged the host in earnest conversation. Turning to his guests, the Doctor remarked,

"Gentlemen, let me present my most intimate friend. I had given specific orders that we were not to be disturbed, but this friend has come to me with an appeal which I cannot decline. His only child is desperately ill. I regret leaving you to your own resources for a time, but I am sure that you will understand. Please excuse me."

Accompanying his friend, the Doctor found the infant in a critical condition. The Doctor had cared for this child since birth, and had also furnished the wetnurse, as the mother had not been able to nurse the child. In spite of his exhilarated condition, the Doctor made a careful examination of the baby, but at first he could not explain what had happened to make it unconscious. At last he diagnosed the situation.

"Bill," he said, "fetch me the wet nurse."

Presently the friend returned, saying that the nurse could not put in an appearance, as she was quite ill.

"I thought so," said the Doctor. "I will go to her. I have an idea."

He found the wet nurse quite unconscious from drink.

"There," said the Doctor, "you have the explanation. The nurse is quite drunk; the child has been fed with her intoxicating milk, and will soon sleep it off." Then he laughed consciously. "As a matter of fact, Bill," he added, "if I had not been drinking myself, I doubt if I should have made the correct diagnosis!"

EPILOGUE

JOHN H CUNNINGHAM

*I*T is permissible, so I am told by my literary friends, for an author to close his volume with philosophical observations. I have been impressed by certain abstract truths that have been revealed to me while refreshing my memory of instances in the years covered in this volume of miscellany. Others before me have, of course, discovered the same truths; but it seems worthwhile to call attention to them here. One great surprise that comes from expressing oneself in print is the uncovering of so many half-truths in his philosophy. In carrying them through to their logical conclusion he adds no small development to his personal understanding. Notable among them is the primary fact that when the boys of my period did wrong, they knew it was wrong. They expected to be punished if they were caught, and stoically accepted their punishment as something they deserved. In this give and take there came an added respect for parents and elders, which would have been destroyed by lack of family discipline.

I have no desire to stamp myself an "old fogey" by comparing present conditions unfavorably with those of my day, but as I read these records consecutively, I am deeply impressed by the contrast. Far be it from me to approve conventions for convention's sake, but I can't help wondering what would have happened to me if the present loose family relations had been in effect when I was a boy. Parental discipline, and the resulting wholesome respect from children for parents, still seem to me to be of fundamental importance even though- today they seem to have passed into the discard.

At present high ideals of all sorts are becoming rather mythical, and in their place we have the "modern attitude" which the younger generation calls "progress." In the old days, the home was for the parents. The children were provided for, made comfortable, and given opportunities for development. Somehow one feels that the youth of the present age take everything for granted. The modern household is run not for the parents but for the children. Regulation of youth by high standards in the home seems to be almost a thing of the past.

I am told by young people who honor me with their confidence that things are now different, and that moral and ethical standards naturally have become changed with "progress." They seem to feel that the regimentation of their lives through the influence of the home cramps their activities, and the acceptance of this view by their parents has caused the influence of the home to drop so low that any regimentation by home influence is now as rare as the Dodo bird.

Why should we place the responsibility of this radical change in family relationships upon the children? There was no member of "Our Gang" who would not gleefully have wrested the authority from his parents if such an incredible idea had ever occurred to him. We accepted the fact that our elders knew more than we did because we really believed it. Is the explanation perhaps that this "modern generation" idea has also infected the parents? There certainly has been a change in them as well as in their offspring. Moral and ethical standards are different. What in my day was called "immorality" is now classified as "unconventionality," and is practiced in the open. There is an acceptance of the French alibi that "Immorality is more moral if expressed without effort to conceal." Personally, I can't help feeling that departures from recognized precedent are better carried out "behind screens" in order that there may still exist a criterion by which to distinguish between right and wrong.

While the parents of my generation were strict in demanding proper conduct from youth, a high sense of respect existed in the relationship of one parent to another. In those days the male felt a serious sense of responsibility in providing for the household, and in making for himself an honorable position in his community. The female had an equally serious sense of responsibility in maintaining the home as a place of comfort for her husband, and in providing a healthful environment for the children. The husband's consideration for his wife led him to respect her finer senses m every way.

Relaxation came to the head of the household only as a reward for accomplishment; there was a general feeling that the pleasures of leisure or sporting pastimes could not be legitimately enjoyed until a man had achieved a commanding position in the community. Even then, successful men asked themselves whether such pursuits as shooting or fishing or apparently wasting time in any way were perhaps unjustifiable as providing a poor example to others who had not "arrived." Impulses were suppressed for ideals. There were two groups of people, one smaller than the other. This latter group included those that were talked about because they occupied high positions; the other group, the great majority, was constituted by those who talked about them. Today there exists this same division of people, the only difference being that the standards of both groups are on a much lower moral and ethical plane.

Just why those who possess the greatest advantages, chiefly through inheritance and opportunity, permit their standards to be lowered, is difficult to understand. As a result, it is inevitable that in the future those less well born and with fewer natural advantages by inheritance, but disciplined in their homes chiefly by economic necessities, will naturally filch the desirable positions from those who have been neglectful of their opportunities.

In my time no young man even thought of marriage until he had proved his mettle, stood on his own feet, had money in the bank, and had assimilated a sense of responsibility in creating his own home. There was a very definite distinction made between the "girlfriend" and the woman chosen to "put her legs under the mahogany table" in the home. There was a rather general realization that "beauty might strike the fancy" but that "merit wins the soul."

My sympathetic friend, Dr. John C. Phillips, tersely expresses the attitude of the present generation as "all over our heads," and suggests that ours may properly be considered the "lost generation." I regretfully agree with him that national regimentation may be our only hope for youth now that the family influence has dropped so low that home discipline is not paramount. Personally, I would rather have my activities regimented by the home influence which develops self-respect, than by a government regimentation which destroys it. This latter seems at the moment to be the ultimate fate of modern youth who think they are securing freedom by "Progress."

Incidentally, speaking of Parents in the broadest sense, those "parents" of industry, the employees of which may properly be called their children, do not seem to be giving their children the same consideration and family help as was the case a generation ago. At the moment of this writing the failure of the "parents'" regimentation of their particular industries to create a happy industrial family relationship, is facing a serious economic problem; and the air seems to be charged with the necessity of government regimentation of the "parents" who have neglected this filial guidance through lowering of moral and ethical business standards for personal economic gain.

"As the twig is bent, the tree's inclined." It must have been made evident in the preceding pages that in my case, the twig was bent in many directions, but fortunately, through the understanding of family environment, was always cultivated in a soil so rich in nourishment that it remained healthy and was never uprooted by winds that twisted it in threatening directions. This is my opportunity to record my gratitude for that understanding. As the twig grows and becomes a sapling, cultivation of the soil and "stresses" to keep it in a certain direction determine its final state of maturity.

This is where the guiding influence of the home comes in, which holds the growth of the twig in an upright position. If these "stresses" are not properly applied, or if the twig is bent in the wrong direction and the defect is not noticed early, later attempts to straighten it out so that it may grow up into the sunlight usually result in only partial accomplishment. As the twig develops into the adult tree, it must still be kept in an upright position to gather the nourishment from the sunlight. The upright tree has the advantage of being able to exercise its normal functions in a normal way, while that which attains maturity by devious means is at a distinct disadvantage.

Nothing is ever attained except by work, which is a normal function of all living things. The work of the home in placing the "guys" on the sapling and pegging these "guys" in the earth to determine the proper direction for further growth, is the responsibility of parents. The parents reap the reward for their efforts in the satisfaction that comes in watching the successful growth of their "twig." The matured tree, in expressing its normal functions increases in strength and eventually forms a protective shade for the parents. Nothing except what is accomplished by work gives satisfaction. One who fishes in waters where a fish is taken on almost every cast, soon loses the thrill of the sport; but he who works all day, exercising his ability in testing various schemes of ingenious technique, and as a result outwits the evasive fish, enjoys keen satisfaction from his work. All work is competitive, no matter in what field.

Success is like a pyramid, larger at the bottom than at the top, with various gradations in size as the top is approached. The theoretical goal of ambition is to sit on top of that pyramid. The space here is limited, and to attain the pinnacle one must climb from the great base through the ever-narrowing approach. This struggle involves work, but with each step upward there comes a sense of satisfaction in realizing that the goal is nearer. This satisfaction is not lessened by the fact that the higher one climbs the more effort is required to advance the remaining distance. In his natural fatigue, one may rest occasionally in the ascent, but if he sleeps in his rest, or ceases his labor in the achievement of the last stretch of this most difficult climb, he may remain on the lower level, with the mortification of seeing those with more determined purpose pass by him.

With every step toward the top of the pyramid, the horizon becomes broader, and one sees things that were not visible from the lower levels. One who has striven to gain the top of his particular pyramid finds there others who have successfully attained the same point. Naturally, there is a community of interests between those on the top just as there is in associations among those who find themselves established on the lower levels, and who look up with envy or appreciation at those at the top. The pyramids of Life vary in size. Some are high and some less so, but all are pyramids, nevertheless. To attain the peak, even of a small pyramid, is an outstanding accomplishment, as it represents healthy accomplishment.

To have a definite object is essential in all work, but one should never strive for a point which is obviously unattainable. Direction is all-important. It is futile to walk on the railroad ties between two parallel tracks which stretch in a straight line for a great distance, and which converge to a false point far out ahead. No matter how faithfully one works to attain this objective, it will always remain ahead and be out of his reach because it is not a real but a false goal.

From my own standpoint, the outstanding features of life are primarily expressed in terms of health, with the resulting energy directed in many different ways, but steered ultimately in the right direction by the influence of the home and the old-fashioned insistence of discipline and respect to elders and applause for accomplishment.

Few "twigs" exposed to natural and unnatural influences remain straight at all times, but guiding influences determine the direction of their ultimate growth.

In the final analysis, "As The Twig is Bent, the Tree's Inclined."

BACK TO SCHOOL & MORE

I stayed on active duty longer than I needed. However, while in the Coast Guard, I got a paycheck and medical benefits. Since North and I were married in December of 1970, it was nice to have that income through most of 1971. We were back on our home turf and had a small cottage that we rented. North was a teacher at Charles River School in Dover.

We had known each other for quite a while as our families were friends, lived near each other in Dover and our fathers were involved in a syndicate that leased a salmon river in Iceland. We started dating after our mutual friend, Spider Andresen's, wedding. It was a time when quite a few of our friends were getting married. We had a June to December engagement and were married just prior to Christmas. I was 25 and North was 23. It was quite common for couples to marry when they were younger than they seem to be today. I know that we looked at our children when they were 25 and 23 and we simply thought, OMG, how did we ever make it? The time was different. There was a war going on and a lot of disruption in the United States. North's mother and father got married in the early days of World War II and her mother was 18. Different time for sure.

My plan had always been to return to graduate school and get a Master of Business Administration degree. Babson College had a very respected program and one that focused on entrepreneurship. It was a perfect fit all around. A 15-minute commute from our home and a year-round program that would allow me to finish up in 18 months. One of the benefits of having been in the military was the Veteran's Administration (VA). As long as I maintained good grades, the VA foot the bill for my graduate education. Not only did I maintain good grades, but I was also able to keep an A average for my time at Babson and was elected to the Beta Gamma Sigma Scholarship Society. Certainly, a great honor, but that and $5 will get you a cup of coffee at Starbucks.

Early on at Rollins, I had thought that I would work to become an architect. The college had a joint program with Columbia University which entailed 3 years at Rollins and an equal number at Columbia. As I took the requisite courses and investigated the program, I found that I would be the first person to complete it. So that was shelved by the end of my freshman year. While in grad school, I focused on real estate development. Same general field as architecture, but instead of designing buildings it would be building them.

While at Babson, I met a number of active-duty Army officers who were at Babson to learn administrative skills. There were about 10 of them and due to the continued unrest from the Vietnam War, they had a separate room where they had meals and did study groups. Through meeting them and having them learn of my recent discharge from active duty, I was invited to join them. One officer became a good friend, George Akin. He was a Lieutenant Colonel at that time and an interesting person. He and his wife visited us in Duxbury at North's parent's house. George loved to fish and catching his first big bluefish was great excitement. He would go on the become a General and had a stellar career that benefited from his time at Babson.

I never attended my graduation from Babson College. It is another thing that I did not do and regret that I did not. I finished up early in the year of 1972 and graduation was in May. I just never connected the events.

Leaving Babson and having to find a real job was not a walk in the park. After a number of interviews, it seemed that I would need some experience in real estate and the most direct avenue appeared to be brokerage. So, I took a course and got my broker's license. I finally got a chance to get a foot in the door with a nascent real estate development company. They had a single large project beginning in conjunction with an established golf course. The plan was to develop apartments first. Then move into single family housing and possibly condominiums. The plan was ok. The execution was problematic.

While more management than development, I got to check the books for the golf course operation every month to see how things were going in comparison to the plan. Usually not too good. I also got a lesson in what restaurants and bars experience with slippage. Some was figured in and it varied plus or minus every month. It was not possible to make it go away, just to manage it.

The bigger problem was the construction side for the apartments. The building with the sales units was done on time, so the leasing effort could start. However, the ongoing construction started to fall behind. The company president, and there were really only two of us, would go out to the site and read the riot act to the construction foreman. That did nothing to speed things up. If anything, it slowed it down. Some days, the foreman would be so mad, he'd simply stop work. My unassigned job became going out to the worksite and calming folks down by agreeing with the foreman that my boss was being a complete jerk. Things were still behind, but at least some work progressed. This routine became so common that it began to wear on me, just as I began to get an understanding of the development process.

Early in the summer of 1973 I had lunch with my Old Farm Road friend Spider Andresen. Spider was working at Salt Water Sportsman magazine and having some fun earning a living in the sport fishing world. I complained about the problems that I constantly had to deal with. About 2 weeks later Spider called me up and said that Kib Bramhall the Advertising Director had decided to retire that he would be taking Kib's job. There would be an opening in the editorial department. Was I interested? Interested, yes, but I needed some time to commit. After thinking about it and discussing the move with North, I decided that

I could always go back to real estate. This would be a once in a lifetime opportunity. I interviewed and got the job and never looked back. The fact that I had written some articles for the magazine while in graduate school didn't hurt, but the biggest plus was my knowledge of fishing.

How well I will always remember my first day. I was sitting at my desk in an area outside the publisher's office in which the Senior Editor sat when he came in to the city. He was an early adopter of remote work at home. Frank Woolner was a very interesting character. He almost always wore a military style beret to the city. He constantly had a pipe clenched between his teeth and was a man of relatively few spoken words. He could write like nobody's business, but he never graduated from high school. He was a New England champion bicycle racer; a WWII military war correspondent; and if you could start almost any poem from memory, he would finish it from memory. He was well read and remembered just about everything that he read.

As he walked by my desk, he tossed a manilla envelope at me. "Read these rejection letters and learn how to write them." The first one I looked at was to a guy I knew from doing public relations for the Coast Guard Auxiliary. It read, "Dear Arnie, This is the worst f#%&ing manuscript I have ever seen. Sorry to see that your camera was also dunked under salt water. Sincerely, Frank Woolner." It took me a long while to stop laughing.

Learning the ins and outs of publishing a monthly magazine was fun. In those early days, it was also very labor intensive. Much was done by hand, and everything had to fit just right. Sometimes, it required a number of tries to make it work. But we usually got it done. We had no computers. We used typewriters. Articles had to be read, edited and sent out for print setting. Each article had to be designed with selected photos. Titles crafted and type set. All that was pasted into place with the advertising and had to fit into numbers of pages that had to be divisible by 4. That was when the magazine was only black and white. Shortly, we added color for articles and advertisements. This meant we had to get all the different page forms correct. There were any number of times where we had to build then take apart and build again into the middle of the night as we were on a deadline. In those early days, so much was manual that my guess is close to two dozen people would touch the product before it went to the printer. When I finally left the company, computers had taken over and the whole process was done by 2 people. In my final days, we proofed everything on a screen and never had a physical product until the magazine was done. Our printers told us about the process changing around the time we bought the magazine. I thought that they were crazy. I was oh so wrong!

Just a few months after I went to work, Frank Woolner was diagnosed with colon cancer. He had surgery and a long recovery. If one had known Frank well, it was obvious that he never really recovered mentally. He completely stopped coming to the office. So, there I was the new guy on the block and the entire editing and layout process was in my hands. I wanted that first magazine to be perfect. Unfortunately, it was not. When the magazine came out and was delivered to Frank's house, I got a call. "What the hell is Stategy?" One article was about West Coast salmon fishing and it was titled "Salmon Strategy." The "R" was left out at type setting. I should have caught it, but I read right by it. My bad, for sure.

Spider and I were pretty much on our own to position the content of the magazine and to sell the advertising. We both felt that the future was with fishing from boats and over time we phased out all the shore-based fishing articles. While it made some folks unhappy, it was the correct decision. Most of the readers were going into boat fishing and that was where the biggest percentage of the advertising funds were being spent.

In 1980, we purchased the magazine from Hal Lyman. It was a bigger task than we had anticipated. Within the first month, the printing company who had historically allowed Hal to be 3 months in arrears on the printing bill came to us with their hand out. They wanted us current and our monthly bill ran in the hundreds of thousands of dollars. I made the gesture of handing them the keys and said, "It's all yours, good luck." They quickly changed their tune to, "Let's figure something out." We did and within a year we were current and never in arrears again.

By chance, we made a darn good team. Spider was the salesman's salesman. He could sell ice to the Eskimos, and they would be happy to buy it. I oversaw the editorial product and took care of the business issues. We also were lucky enough to have been in a boom time for fishing and boating. We built the publication with a first class product on a foundation of good information from the best in the salt water fishing world. Our audience was dedicated and so was our staff. We always tried to hire fishermen first. We could teach the editing and writing process, but the subject knowledge was priceless. Within a few years, we had built the largest salt water fishing publication in the world. It was as much fun as you can have while working, but it required a lot of time. In a fairly short while, I became a multiple million miler on Delta Airlines. We traveled to shows around the country. We traveled to see major advertisers. We traveled to learn new fishing areas and to entertain important advertising clients.

After owning and building the company for about eight years, we began to get inquiries about our interest in selling. At first we pushed back. But then we sat down and put our heads together on the idea. Soon, the serious offers started to chase us. Finally in 1988, we took an offer from the Times Mirror Company to join their magazine division. We knew the CEO, who was an avid angler. It was a great deal with a very good company. Our staff was greatly concerned, but the Times Mirror managers were true to their word and left us alone to do our thing. We not only had the magazine, but we had also built a very good mail order business and the most successful fishing education seminar series.

We continued to grow the company for about another six months and then the economy started to slow down. Suddenly, we were grateful that we had made the decision we did. Unfortunately, it is never the same working for someone else rather than yourself. It became apparent that the company would not keep both of us on. So, Spider and I sat down and talked. I said that I would retire, and he could run the show. No, he said that he was having a hard time adjusting to the big company mentality and that he would be the one to retire.

That was in 1992 and I managed to hang on for another 12 years. I liked what I was doing even if I had to tell my NY managers that they had no idea what they were doing. In 2004, I was blindsided by the new owners of the company. I did not so much mind the fact that I was being let go, since I knew it would happen sooner or later. However, a 30 second dismissal after 30 plus years is just disrespectful. The only plus is that without them throwing me out the door, I'd likely still be there. I loved what I did and as the saying goes, due to that I never worked a day in my life.

Now you know most of the first of the story.

Colin M "Rip" Cunningham Jr.

EPILOGUE

Looking back on all those years of growing up, I cannot say that I spent much time thinking about the process. However, since then, I have thought a lot about those years. While there is the good, the bad and the ugly, I can honestly say that they were mostly good. Those formative years are fun and exciting. Without doubt, I was lucky enough to be able to experience a lot of different things, maybe too many, which made me into a kind of jack of many trades and a master of none. Well, I could fish and shoot pretty darn well, and that is a good start. I doubt that I was different than most kids my age growing up. Not really having a solid idea of where I wanted to go with my life. Some say they want to be a doctor or a fireman or maybe the President of the United States, but those are few and far between. I was not one of them by any stretch of the imagination.

Mostly, we just move through our young lives with direction from our parents and secondarily from our friends. At some point in our lives, peers become more influential than parents. I was very lucky in some of the most important decisions in my life and I'd rather be lucky than good. I was most fortunate to have found North to be the person to march hand and hand with me. The next step is finding our own direction and building a life around that. One of the ideas that my grandfather, Dr. Cunningham, was very insistent about was that it mattered less what you want to do with your life. However, what was most important was to be the best possible version of whatever you wanted to be. I tried to follow that advice.

In thinking about all that has happened in my lifetime, I can honestly say that what I regret the most is not having done some things. Not taking my studies more seriously up through high school level is certainly something that I'd do differently. Would that have materially changed my life? I have no idea. However, I do know that it would have given me more opportunities. It would certainly have not been a bad thing.

At college, where my studies excelled, I regret not having stayed on the crew for all four years. My first two years rowing were very gratifying. During the summer between freshman and sophomore years, my back injury from doing rough landscaping work with a friend as a summer job never completely healed. For the sophomore year rowing was harder and my back a constant problem. My only response was dropping out of crew. Looking back, the injury was at least partially due to the lack of strength training and physical fitness regimens in high school and college. Today strength training is the norm and very beneficial. While my back issues stayed with me for the rest of my life, having had some help with working through that injury would have been a plus and might have been helpful for a long time.

When I joined the Coast Guard, I had recently earned my pilot's license. I expressed some interest in the Coast Guard flight program and was given the aptitude test for flight school. I scored very high. For several months, I received a letter or phone call at least once a week to ask when I was applying for flight school. The calculation that I made was if I wanted to make a career of the Coast Guard, the extra time required for and after flight school would be fine. However, I felt that I wanted to do something else with the rest of my life and turned down the offer. I often regret that decision. I always found flying to be exciting and challenging. While I had learned to fly fixed wing aircraft, I will always regret not learning how to fly rotary aircraft (helicopters). To this day, I find them to be amazing machines.

When you get the point in your life where I am now, I suspect that you too will regret the things that you didn't do. And if you do not, then you will have lived a very exciting and fulfilling life. Good on ya, as the Aussies would say.

I chose the name for this book because it had some association with the name that my grandfather selected for his book, *As The Twig Is Bent*, which is being partially reprinted with this book as well.

Where The Acorn Falls was picked because of the old expression "the acorn doesn't fall too far from the tree." That would imply that one's family has a great deal of influence on how one lives their life. My grandfather was a believer in the old adage, "spare the rod and spoil the child." He believed in strict discipline. My parents were nowhere near as strict as my grandfather, but they did believe in discipline when it was deserved, and I did deserve it from time to time. As mentioned previously, the most memorable, because it lasted so long, was when the end of my junior year report card came from Mr. Putnam, Headmaster at Nobles. He wrote on it, "Colin will not go to college unless there is dramatic improvement." My father took it and taped it to my bathroom mirror right where I would look to brush my teeth, wash my face and shave. He said it would stay there until I got into college. It was there for about eight months.

When North and I raised our children, we were less disciplinary than our parents had been, mostly for two reasons. First, our peers were also less disciplinary than the previous generation and that does have some influence. But mostly because North was such a good mother our children did not need a lot of discipline. Only an occasional threat to stop the car when they were fighting during a trip and to throw them out on the side of the road, which quickly became no threat at all just parental bluster. The one time that I did follow through with a disciplinary threat was one Halloween. Both children had returned home from trick or treating with grocery bags full of candy. Then as each dumped their load on the family room floor, fighting broke out over items the other had in their pile. I warned that if it persisted, I'd throw the whole mess in the wood stove. It continued and they watched in total amazement when I pitched both bags into the wood stove. They were dumbfounded, but almost had the last laugh. Sugar burns and once going does so with vigor. I had to run outside and look at the chimney which looked like a roman candle with sparks and flames shooting out. Luckily, by damping down the wood stove to restrict the oxygen needed by the chimney fire, it quickly subsided. Both of our children remember that to this day and probably have not forgiven me.

Where The Acorn Falls also refers to the natural world where the acorn does not tend to fall too far from the tree that grew it. Some will fall and lay fallow, producing nothing. Others will become fodder for the surrounding critters, and some will find fertile ground and grow into a mighty oak. In many ways, a metaphor for how our lives transpire.

As I look back over the years, there are things that I would certainly have done differently, and chances taken that luckily worked out well. How well I remember starting out in the real estate world. Then after that my old friend, Spider Andresen, from the Dedham gang got me interested in trying magazine publishing with Salt Water Sportsman. I agonized about making the change and finally took the leap. We were able to build what had been a respected small magazine into the biggest salt water sport fishing publishing company in the world. I loved what I did and due to that I never worked a day in my life. Is there luck involved, you bet there is. But the reality is that you make most of your luck by building the right thing, in the right place, at the right time.

I have said this before, but it bears repeating. The things that I most regret in life are things that I did not do. Sure, there are plenty of things that I have done that I regret, but those were generally passing remorse. In closing, I'll reprint a poem by my favorite poet Robert Frost, "The Road Not Taken." It says it all.

Two roads diverged in a yellow wood,
And sorry I could not travel both
And be one traveler, long I stood
And looked down one as far as I could
To where it bent in the undergrowth;

Where the Acorn Falls

Then took the other, as just as fair,
And having perhaps the better claim,
Because it was grassy and wanted wear;
Though as for that the passing there
Had worn them really about the same,
And both that morning equally lay
In leaves no step had trodden black.
Oh, I kept the first for another day!
Yet knowing how way leads on to way,
I doubted if I should ever come back.
I shall be telling this with a sigh
Somewhere ages and ages hence:
Two roads diverged in a wood, and I—
I took the one less traveled by,
And that has made all the difference.

ACKNOWLEDGEMENTS

This has been a fun undertaking. Searching the corners of my memory for information long set aside to make room for more of life's adventure. When I wasn't sure about some details, I went to others to get their recollection of what transpired. Some of the Old Farm Road gang came through as I knew they would. Spider Andresen thankfully (from my perspective) had firsthand knowledge of the ski boot tackle. Phil Reed and Mimi Reed Plumb helped with some missing details of the Blue Angel bicycle escapades and other two wheeled adventure. Clint Smith chimed in on a variety of details. Thanks to Russell Cleary for digging up photographic memories of life aboard the *Jaguar*. Unfortunately, some of the gang have gone to the other side and if I have blotted my copy book, I am sure that I will hear about it in the great beyond.

Thanks to all for being friends. We grew up in a wonderful time to be a kid in this country.

Writing a book is only part of the process. Taking the words and crafting them into an attractive, pleasing and functional product takes patience and talent. My sincere thanks to Wally and Betty Turnbull of Light Messages/Torch Flame Books for their valuable help.

ABOUT THE AUTHOR

Rip Cunningham grew up around the water and has had a direct connection to a lot of its finned residents. He was the Editor-In-Chief/Publisher/Owner of *Salt Water Sportsman*, at that time the largest saltwater sport fishing magazine in the world. For the last 50 years, he has written hundreds of articles for a number of titles on fishing techniques, fisheries management and conservation.
He continues to be the Conservation Editor of *Salt Water Sportsman*.

    Rip received a BA from Rollins College and an MBA from Babson College. He has been appointed to state and federal fishery management commissions and councils. In 2015, he was inducted into the Fishing Hall of Fame.

    Having fished on almost every continent and ocean, he is now focused on trying to make sure common property fish resources are here for generations to come. He is dedicated to using all of his lifelong experience to leave the world a little bit better place with sustainable resources for all to enjoy, especially his grandchildren.

Colin M "Rip" Cunningham Jr.

Rip and his wife, North, live part-time along the coast of Maine and part-time in the woods of Massachusetts, where their seven grandchildren command attention.

Follow Rip:
facebook.com/ripcham11
x.com/ripcham11

Printed in the USA
CPSIA information can be obtained
at www.ICGtesting.com
CBHW060957170124
3506CB00011B/1219